D0464295

The Political Participation of Women in the United States:

A Selected Bibliography,

1950-1976

CENTER FOR
THE AMERICAN WOMAN AND POLITICS
Eagleton Institute of Politics
Rutgers University

Kathy Stanwick
and
Christine Li

The Scarecrow Press, Inc.
Metuchen, N.J. & London
1977

Library of Congress Cataloging in Publication Data

Stanwick, Kathy.
  The political participation of women in the United
States.

  Includes indexes.
  1. Women in politics--United States--Bibliography.
I. Li, Christine, joint author. II. Rutgers Uni-
versity, New Brunswick, N. J. Center for the American
Woman and Politics. III. Title.
Z7961.S74   [HQ1236]   016.3015'92'0973   77-23036
ISBN 0-8108-1075-1

ABOUT THE CENTER

The Center for the American Woman and Politics (CAWP) is a unique research, education, and service center working to increase knowledge about women's participation in public life. As part of the Eagleton Institute of Politics at Rutgers University, CAWP programs reflect Eagleton's interest in political institutions, political practitioners, and public policy in the United States.

The Center believes in encouraging the full and effective involvement of women in American public affairs. National in scope, Center programs support the growth and strength of a truly representative government responsive to the needs of all citizens, female and male alike.

CAWP activities include developing educational programs, generating and sponsoring research, convening conferences and symposia, and publishing and disseminating information. By designing and sponsoring a variety of programs, the Center serves a catalytic role in the development of important information about women's participation in government and politics.

Established in 1971 with the aid of a Ford Foundation grant to the Eagleton Institute, the Center for the American Woman and Politics seeks additional funds to support its programs. Neither CAWP nor the Eagleton Institute of Politics is a lobbying organization. All programs undertaken by the Center and the Institute are nonpartisan, and all donations are tax exempt.

Center Staff

Ruth B. Mandel, Director
Marilyn Johnson, Director of Research
Kathy Stanwick, Research and Information Associate
Ruth Ann Burns, Program Associate
Nancy Becker, Program Consultant
Christine Li, Project Assistant
Patricia DeCandia, Secretary
Maryjane Davies, Secretary

CONTENTS

PREFACE

A major goal of the Center for the American Woman and Politics (CAWP) is to increase knowledge about the political life of women in the United States. In pursuing this aim, CAWP regularly monitors published writings and on-going research on the subject. The Political Participation of Women in the United States: A Selected Bibliography 1950-1976 is the result of a systematic attempt to assemble citations to all materials available on American women's political participation at both mass and elite levels.

The more than 1,500 entries in this bibliography represent continued expansion and updating of the compilation issued by CAWP in 1974, entitled Women and American Politics: A Selected Bibliography, 1965-1974. Since 1974 the number of works concerned with women's political activity has increased markedly. Yet the existing material constitutes only a beginning in the study and understanding of women's public status and political impact. By enabling educators, researchers and other interested persons to identify easily the scarce and scattered materials about women's roles in the political process of the United States, CAWP aims also to stimulate assessment of gaps in the literature and efforts to fill these gaps through further research and writing.

The bibliography contains references to published and unpublished writings produced in the period 1950 through 1976, as well as references to work in progress. Included is a diversity of types of materials. There are citations to theoretical analyses, reports of research, speculative essays, historical narratives, profiles and biographies, and journalistic accounts of political events involving women. No attempt has been made, however, to include the numerous reports appearing in newspapers, and inclusion of articles from general readership magazines has been highly selective.

The citations are to works that contain information about one or more of the following subjects: women who hold elective or appointive office, and other politically active women; women's roles in the political parties; voting behavior; political socialization; women's lobbying; women's voluntary political activity in both ad hoc and formally organized groups as such activity affects the legislative process and the formation of public policy; women's roles in social movements; historical accounts of the political activities of women. Items which focus on specific social or political issues such as abortion or financial discrimination are included only if they also contain a description or discussion of the political activity of women regarding these issues.

References are grouped according to their format: bibliographies; directories and encyclopedias; periodicals; books, monographs and reports; articles; dissertations and theses; unpublished papers presented at professional meetings; miscellaneous unpublished papers; research in progress. The arrangement is alphabetical by author or by main entry within each category. A biographical index and an author index are supplied to further assist the user. Where unpublished works are known to be available from an author or organization, addresses and prices accompany the citation.

Despite efforts to assure inclusion of all relevant materials, unintentional omissions have almost certainly occurred.

Since knowledge by the Center about work in progress is dependent upon direct communication with CAWP by investigators and their colleagues, the listing of ongoing projects may especially be incomplete. We wish to thank the many individuals who do inform us of their own work and that of their colleagues, and we urge all users of the bibliography to submit to the Center notices of additional relevant materials for listing in future editions.

The specialized collection of materials about women's political participation in the United States maintained at the Center contains many of the items listed in the bibliography. Inquiries are invited regarding use of these materials.

For submission of additional citations and for information regarding use of CAWP's special collection or the availability of particular items, contact:

Kathy Stanwick
    Research and Information Associate
Center for the American Woman and Politics
Eagleton Institute of Politics
Rutgers University
New Brunswick, N. J.   08901
(201) 828-2210

Kathy Stanwick
Research and Information Associate

Christine Li
Project Assistant

February 1977

The Bibliography

BIBLIOGRAPHIES

1 Adams, Ethel M., and Cope, S. D. Volunteers: An
  Annotated Bibliography. New York: United Community Funds and Councils of America, 1968.

2 Astin, Helen S.; Suniewick, Nancy; and Dweck, Susan.
  Women: A Bibliography on Their Education and Careers. Washington, D.C.: Human Service Press,
  1971.

3 Bibliographic Information Center. Women in Politics:
  Toward a Bibliography of Bibliographies. (The Bib-
  liographic Information Center, 2570 Sue Avenue, San
  Jose, Calif. 95111)

4 Center for the American Woman and Politics. Voluntary
  Participation Among Women in the United States: A
  Selected Bibliography, 1950-1976. New Brunswick,
  N.J.: Rutgers University, Eagleton Institute of Poli-
  tics, 1976.

5 _____. Women and American Politics: A Selected
  Bibliography, 1965-1974. New Brunswick, N.J.:
  Rutgers University, Eagleton Institute of Politics,
  1974.

6 Cisler, Lucinda. Women: A Bibliography. 6th ed.
  July-October 1970. (P.O. Box 240, Planetarium Sta-
  tion, New York, N.Y. 10024.) $.50.

7 Cole, Johnneta B. "Black Women in America: An Annotated Bibliography." Black Scholar 3 (December
  1971): 42-53.

8 Davis, Lenwood G. Black Women in Cities: 1872-1972.
  Monticello, Ill.: Council of Planning Librarians,
  1972.

1

9 _____. The Woman in American Society: A Selected
   Bibliography. 2d rev. ed. Monticello, Ill.: Council
   of Planning Librarians, 1975.

10 Developing New Horizons for Women: Bibliography.
   Washington, D.C.: George Washington University
   Press, 1970.

11 Drake, Kirsten; Marks, Dorothy; and Wexford, Mary.
   Women's Work and Women's Studies, 1971. New
   York: The Women's Center, Barnard College, 1972.

12 Felmley, Jenrose. Working Women: Homemakers and
   Volunteers. Washington, D.C.: Business and Professional Women's Foundation, 1975.

13 Fitch, Nancy. Women in Politics: The United States
   and Abroad. A Selected Bibliography. Washington,
   D.C.: Library of Congress, Congressional Research
   Service, Government Division, 1976.

14 Freeman, Leah. The Changing Role of Women: A Selected Bibliography. Bibliographic Series No. 9.
   Sacramento: California State College Library, 1970.

15 _____. The Changing Role of Women: A Selected
   Bibliography. Rev. ed. Bibliographic Series No. 9.
   Sacramento: California State University Library,
   1972.

16 Friedman, Barbara, et al., eds. Women's Work and
   Women's Studies/1973-1974: A Bibliography. New
   York: Barnard College Women's Center, 1975. (Dis-
   tributed by The Feminist Press, Old Westbury, N.Y.)

17 Jacobs, Sue-Ellen. Women in Cross-Cultural Perspective: A Preliminary Sourcebook. Illinois: University
   of Illinois, Department of Urban and Regional Planning, 1971.

18 Krichmar, Albert. The Women's Rights Movement in
   the United States, 1848-1970: A Bibliography and
   Sourcebook. Metuchen, N.J.: Scarecrow Press,
   1972.

19 Levenson, Rosaline. Women in Government and Politics:
   A Bibliography of American and Foreign Sources. Ex-

change Bibliography 491. Monticello, Ill. : Council
of Planning Librarians, 1973.

20 Levitt, Morris. Women's Role in American Politics.
Exchange Bibliography 446. Monticello, Ill. : Council
of Planning Librarians, 1973.

21 Loventhal, Milton. Autobiographies of Women, 1946-
1970: A Bibliography. San Jose, Calif. : San Jose
State College Library, 1972.

22 O'Connor, Patricia. Women: A Selected Bibliography.
Springfield, Ohio: Wittenberg University, Woman and
the Human Revolution, 1973.

23 Rosenberg, Marie Barovic, and Bergstrom, Len V. , eds.
Women and Society: A Critical Review of the Litera-
ture with a Selected Annotated Bibliography. Beverly
Hills, Calif. : Sage, 1975.

24 Sapiro, Virginia. A Guide to Published Works on Women and Politics II. Ann Arbor: University of Michigan, Institute for Social Research, Center for Political Studies, 1975.

25 Schuman, Pat, and Detlefsen, Gay. "Sisterhood Is Seri-
ous--An Annotated Bibliography." Library Journal
96 (September 1971): 2587-2594.

25a Soltow, Martha Jane, and Wery, Mary K. American
Women and the Labor Movement, 1825-1974: An An-
notated Bibliography. Metuchen, N. J. : Scarecrow
Press, 1976.

26 United States. Department of Labor. Women's Bureau.
American Women at the Crossroads: Directions for
the Future. Washington, D. C. , 1970.

27 _____. Library of Congress. Legislative Reference
Service. The New Feminism: An Annotated Reading
List. Washington, D. C. , 1970.

28 Wai-hing Lo, Henrietta. Women's Studies: A Bibliography. Chico: California State University, 1973.

29 Whaley, Sara Stauffer. "American Women in National
Political Life." Women's Studies Abstracts 1 (spring
1972): 1.

30   Wheeler, Helen. Womanhood Media: Current Resources About Women. Metuchen, N.J.: Scarecrow Press, 1972.

31   _____. Womanhood Media Supplement: Additional Current Resources About Women. Metuchen, N.J.: Scarecrow Press, 1975.

32   Wollter, Patricia. 50 Years After the 19th Amendment: A Bibliography on the Elusive Struggle for Women's Liberation. Rohnert Park, Calif.: Sonoma State College Library, 1971.

33   Young, Louise M. "The American Woman at Mid-Century: Bibliographical Essay." American Review 11 (December 1961): 121-138.

DIRECTORIES AND ENCYCLOPEDIAS

34 Barrer, Myra E., ed. Women's Organizations &
    Leaders Directory--1975-1976 Edition. Washington,
    D.C.: Today Publications & News Service, 1975.

35 Center for the American Woman and Politics. Women
    in Public Office: A Biographical Directory and Sta-
    tistical Analysis. New York: R. R. Bowker, 1976.

36 Encyclopedia of Associations. 3 vols. Detroit: Gale
    Research Company. Annual.

37 James, Edward T., ed. Notable American Women 1607-
    1950: A Biographical Dictionary. Three Volumes.
    Cambridge, Mass.: Harvard University Press,
    Belknap Press, 1971.

PERIODICALS

38 Barrer, Myra E., ed. <u>Journal of Reprints of Documents</u>
    <u>Affecting Women.</u> Washington, D.C.: Today Publica-
    tions & News Service. Quarterly.

39 Crater, Flora, ed. <u>The Woman Activist: An Action</u>
    <u>Bulletin for Women's Rights.</u> Falls Church, Va.:
    The Woman Activist, Inc. Monthly.

40 Feminist Action Alliance, Inc. <u>Inter-Action.</u> Atlanta, Ga.
    Monthly.

41 Flynn, Sharon, ed. <u>Women's Political Times.</u> Washing-
    ton, D.C.: National Women's Political Caucus, Inc.
    Bi-monthly.

42 Forbes, Carol, ed. <u>Congressional Clearinghouse on</u>
    <u>Women's Rights.</u> Washington, D.C. Weekly (when
    Congress is in session).

43 Hogan, Betsy, ed. <u>Womanpower.</u> 222 Rawson Road,
    Brookline, Mass. Monthly.

44 Hosken, Fran P., ed. <u>Women's International Network</u>
    <u>(WIN) News.</u> 187 Grant Street, Lexington, Mass.
    Quarterly.

45 League of Women Voters. <u>The National Voter.</u> Wash-
    ington, D.C. Bi-monthly.

46 Lee, Douglas, ed. <u>Winning Spirit.</u> Washington, D.C.:
    National Federation of Republican Women. Monthly
    (may vary).

47 Majority Report, Inc. <u>Majority Report.</u> New York.
    Bi-weekly.

48 Moore, Barbara Jordan, ed. <u>Women Today.</u> Washing-
    ton, D.C.: Today Publications & News Service,
    Inc. Bi-monthly.

49 Ms. Magazine Corporation. <u>Ms.</u> New York. Monthly.

50 National Women's Political Caucus. <u>Republican Women's Task Force Newsletter</u>. Washington, D. C. Monthly (may vary).

51 Smith, David Horton, ed. <u>Journal of Voluntary Action Research</u>. Chestnut Hill, Mass.: Association of Voluntary Action Scholars. Quarterly.

52 Stimpson, Catharine R., ed. <u>Signs: Journal of Women in Culture and Society</u>. Chicago: University of Chicago Press. Quarterly.

53 Sweet, Ellen B., ed. <u>Women's Agenda</u>. New York: Women's Action Alliance. Ten times yearly.

54 Tenenbaum, Susan, ed. <u>Women's Washington Representative: A Women's Legislative Service</u>. Washington, D. C. Monthly.

55 Wellisch, Karen, ed. <u>The Spokeswoman: A Crossroads of Communication for Women</u>. Chicago. Monthly.

56 Women's Equity Action League. <u>WEAL Washington Report</u>. Washington, D. C. Monthly.

BOOKS, MONOGRAPHS, AND REPORTS

57   Abzug, Bella S. <u>Bella! Ms. Abzug Goes to Washington.</u>
Edited by Mel Ziegler. New York: Saturday Review
Press, 1972.

58   Adams, Elsie, and Briscoe, Mary Louise. <u>Up Against
the Wall, Mother ... On Women's Liberation.</u>
Beverly Hills, Calif.: Glencoe Press, 1971.

59   Adams, Mildred. <u>The Right to Be People.</u> Philadelphia:
Lippincott, 1967.

60   Agger, Robert E.; Goldrich, Daniel; and Swanson, Bert
E. <u>The Rulers and the Ruled: Political Power and
Impotence in American Communities.</u> New York:
John Wiley, 1964.

61   Aldrich, Darragh. <u>Lady in Law: A Biography of
Mabeth Hurd Paige.</u> Chicago: Ralph Fletcher Seymour, 1950.

62   Almond, Gabriel A., and Verba, Sidney. <u>The Civic
Culture: Political Attitudes and Democracy in Five
Nations.</u> Boston: Little, Brown, 1965.

63   Alpha Kappa Alpha Sorority, Inc. <u>Negro Women in the
Judiciary.</u> Booklet no. 1. Chicago: Alpha Kappa
Alpha Sorority, 1969.

64   _____. <u>Women in Politics.</u> Booklet no. 2. Chicago:
Alpha Kappa Alpha Sorority, July, 1969.

65   Amrine, Michael. <u>The Awesome Challenge.</u> New York:
Putnam, 1964.

66   Amundsen, Kirsten. <u>The Silenced Majority: Women and
American Democracy.</u> Englewood Cliffs, N.J.:
Prentice-Hall, 1971.

67   Anderson, Mary. Woman at Work: The Autobiography
     of Mary Anderson as Told to Mary N. Winslow.
     Minneapolis: University of Minnesota Press, 1951.

68   Andreas, Carol. Sex and Caste in America. Englewood
     Cliffs, N.J.: Prentice-Hall, 1971.

69   Anthony, Katherine. First Lady of the Revolution: A
     Life of Mercy Warren. New York: Doubleday, 1958.

70   _____. Susan B. Anthony: Her Personal History and
     Her Era. New York: Doubleday, 1954.

71   Anticaglia, Elizabeth. Twelve American Women. Chi-
     cago: Nelson-Hall, 1975.

72   Atkins, Martha. The Hidden History of the Female:
     The Early Feminist Movement in the United States.
     Toronto: Hogtown Press, 1971.

73   Atlanta, Georgia, Community Relations Commission.
     Women in City Government: Atlanta, Georgia. 1973.

74   Bach, Patricia G. Women in Public Life in Wisconsin:
     A Preliminary Report. Milwaukee: Alverno College
     Research Center on Women, 1971.

75   Banner, Lois W. Women in Modern America: A Brief
     History. New York: Harcourt Brace Jovanovich,
     1974.

76   Barber, James. Citizen Politics: An Introduction to
     Political Behavior. Chicago: Markham, 1969.

77   Bardwick, Judith M. Psychology of Women: A Study
     of Bio-Cultural Conflicts. New York: Harper and
     Row, 1971.

78   Barone, Michael; Ujifusa, Grant; and Matthews, Douglas.
     The Almanac of American Politics 1976. New York:
     E. P. Dutton, 1975.

79   Bates, Daisy. The Long Shadow of Little Rock. New
     York: David McKay, 1962.

80   Bauer, Raymond A.; de Sola Pool, Ithial; and Dexter,
     Lewis A. American Business and Public Policy:

The Politics of Foreign Trade. Chicago: Aldine-Atherton, 1972.

81 Beal, George M., et al. System Linkages Among Women's Organizations. Ames: Iowa State University, Department of Sociology and Anthropology, 1967.

82 Beard, Mary R. America Through Woman's Eyes. Westport, Conn.: Greenwood Press, 1969.

83 _____. Women as Force in History. New York: Collier, 1962.

84 Bell, Wendell; Hill, Richard J.; and Wright, Charles R. Public Leadership. San Francisco: Chandler, 1961.

85 Bem, Daryl, ed. Beliefs, Attitudes and Human Affairs. Belmont, California: Brooks Cole, 1970.

86 Berelson, Bernard R.; Lazarsfeld, Paul F.; and McPhee, William N. Voting: A Study of Opinion Formation in a Presidential Campaign. Chicago: University of Chicago Press, 1954.

87 Bernard, Jacqueline. Journey Toward Freedom. New York: Dell, 1967.

88 Bernard, Jessie. Academic Women. University Park: Pennsylvania State University Press, 1964.

89 _____. Women and the Public Interest: An Essay on Policy and Protest. Chicago: Aldine-Atherton, 1971.

90 Bird, Caroline, with Briller, Sara W. Born Female: The High Cost of Keeping Women Down. New York: David McKay, 1968.

91 Blumberg, Dorothy R. Florence Kelley: The Making of a Social Pioneer. New York: A. M. Kelley, 1966.

92 Blumenthal, Walter H. American Panorama: Patterns of the Past and Womanhood in Its Unfolding. Worcester, Mass.: Achille J. St. Onge, 1962.

93 Borgese, Elisabeth Mann. Ascent of Woman. New York: George Braziller, 1963.

94 Bosmajian, Hamida, ed. This Great Argument: The
    Rights of Women. New York: Canfield Press,
    1972.

95 Bradford, Sarah H. Scenes in the Life of Harriet
    Tubman, or Harriet Tubman: The Moses of Her
    People. New York: Corinth Books, 1961.

96 Brownmiller, Susan. Shirley Chisholm. Garden City,
    N.Y.: Doubleday, 1970.

97 Burdick, Eugene, and Brodbeck, Arthur J., eds.
    American Voting Behavior. Glencoe, Ill.: Free
    Press, 1959.

98 Burnett, Constance Buel. Five for Freedom: Lucretia
    Mott, Elizabeth Cady Stanton, Lucy Stone, Susan B.
    Anthony, Carrie Chapman Catt. New York: Abe-
    lard Press, 1953.

99 Butler, Phyllis, and Gray, Dorothy. Everywoman's
    Guide to Political Awareness. Millbrae, Calif:
    Les Femmes, 1976.

100 Cade, Toni, ed. The Black Woman: An Anthology.
    New York: Signet, 1970.

101 California Commission on the Status of Women, ed.
    Impact ERA: Limitations and Possibilities. Mill-
    brae, Calif.: Les Femmes, 1976.

102 California Elected Women's Association for Education
    and Research (CEWAER). Organizational Kit. Los
    Angeles, Calif.: CEWAER, 1975.

103 Calisher, Hortense. Herself. New York: Arbor
    House, 1972.

104 Campbell, Angus, and Cooper, Homer C. Group
    Differences in Attitudes and Votes. Ann Arbor:
    University of Michigan, Institute for Social Research,
    Survey Research Center, 1956.

105 _____, and Kahn, Robert L. The People Elect a
    President. Ann Arbor: University of Michigan,
    Institute for Social Research, Survey Research
    Center, 1952.

106 _____; Gurin, Gerald; and Miller, Warren E. The
Voter Decides. Evanston, Ill.: Row, Peterson,
1954.

107 _____, et al. The American Voter. New York:
John Wiley, 1960.

108 Cannon, James, ed. Politics, U.S.A.: A Practical
Guide to the Winning of Public Office. New York:
Doubleday, 1960.

109 Cantril, Albert H., and Cantril, Susan Davis. The
Report of the Findings of the League Self-Study.
Washington, D.C.: League of Women Voters, 1974.

110 Carden, Maren Lockwood. The New Feminist Movement. New York: Russell Sage Foundation, 1974.

111 Carter, Mae R., ed. The Role of Women in Politics.
Newark, Del.: University of Delaware, Division of
Continuing Education, 1974.

112 Cassara, Beverly B., ed. American Women: The
Changing Image. Boston: Beacon Press, 1962.

113 Cater, Libby A.; Scott, Anne Firor; and Martyna,
Wendy. Women and Men: Changing Roles, Rela-
tionships and Perceptions. Palo Alto, California:
Aspen Institute for Humanistic Studies, 1976.

114 Center for the American Woman and Politics. Educating
Women for Public Life: Report from the Visiting
Program in Practical Politics. New Brunswick,
N.J.: Rutgers University, Eagleton Institute of
Politics, 1974.

115 _____. Women Appointed to State Boards and Commissions. New Brunswick, N.J.: Rutgers University, Eagleton Institute of Politics, 1976.

116 _____. Women State Legislators: Report from a
Conference. New Brunswick, N.J.: Rutgers University, Eagleton Institute of Politics, 1973.

117 Chafe, William. The American Woman: Her Changing
Social, Economic, and Political Roles, 1920-1970.
New York: Oxford University Press, 1972.

118   Chamberlin, Hope. A Minority of Members: Women
         in the U.S. Congress. New York: Praeger, 1973.

119   Chester, Giraud. Embattled Maiden: The Life of Anna
         Dickinson. New York: G. P. Putnam, 1951.

120   Chisholm, Shirley. The Good Fight. New York:
         Harper and Row, 1973.

121   _____. Unbought and Unbossed. Boston: Houghton
         Mifflin, 1970.

122   Citizens' Advisory Council on the Status of Women.
         Women in 1971. Washington, D.C.: U.S. Govern-
         ment Printing Office, 1972.

123   _____. Women in 1975. Washington, D.C.:
         Citizens' Advisory Council on the Status of Women,
         1976.

124   Colorado Commission on the Status of Women. See
         How She Runs: A Guide for the Woman Candidate.
         Pueblo: Colorado Commission on the Status of
         Women, 1972.

125   Common Cause. Common Cause Action Program for:
         Ratification of the Equal Rights Amendment. Wash-
         ington, D.C.: Common Cause, 1973.

126   Conference on the Role of the State Commissions on the
         Status of Women in Ten Western States, Portland,
         Oregon. Expanding Women's Effectiveness in the
         Community: A Report. 1968.

127   Congressional Quarterly Editorial Research Reports.
         The Women's Movement. Washington, D.C.: Con-
         gressional Quarterly, 1973.

128   Conrad, Earl. Harriet Tubman: Negro Soldier and
         Abolitionist. New York: International Press, 1968.

129   Conyers, James E., and Wallace, Walter L. Black
         Elected Officials: A Study of Black Americans
         Holding Governmental Office. New York: Russell
         Sage Foundation, 1976.

130   Coolidge, Olivia E. Women's Rights: The Suffrage

Movement in America, 1848-1920. New York:
Dutton, 1966.

131 Cooper, James, and Cooper, Sheila McIsaac. The
     Roots of American Feminism. Boston: Allyn and
     Bacon, 1973.

132 Cott, Nancy F., ed. Root of Bitterness: Documents
     of the Social History of American Women. New
     York: Dutton, 1972.

133 Cotter, Cornelius P., and Hennessy, Bernard C.
     Politics Without Power: The National Party Com-
     mittees. New York: Atherton, 1964.

134 Cromwell, Otelia. Lucretia Mott. Cambridge, Mass.:
     Harvard University Press, 1958.

135 Cutler, John H. What About Women?: An Examination
     of the Present Characteristics, Nature, Status, and
     Position of Women as They Have Evolved During
     This Century. New York: Washburn, 1961.

136 Dahlstrom, Edmund, ed. The Changing Roles of Men
     and Women. Boston: Beacon Press, 1971.

137 Daniels, Arlene Kaplan. A Survey of Research Con-
     cerns on Women's Issues. Washington, D.C.:
     Association of American Colleges, 1975.

138 _____; Eriksson-Joslyn, Kerstin; and Ruzek, Sheryl K.
     The Place of Volunteerism in the Lives of Women:
     Final Report. San Francisco: Scientific Analysis
     Corporation, 1975.

139 Dannett, Sylvia. Profiles of Negro Womanhood. Yon-
     kers, New York: Educational Heritage, 1966.

140 David, Lester. Joan: The Reluctant Kennedy. New
     York: Funk and Wagnalls, 1974.

141 David, Opal D., ed. The Education of Women--Signs
     for the Future. Washington, D.C.: American
     Council on Education, 1959.

142 David, Paul T.; Goldman, Ralph N.; and Bain, Richard
     C. The Politics of National Party Convention.
     Washington, D.C.: Brookings Institution, 1960.

143 Davis, Allen F. American Heroine: The Life and
    Legend of Jane Addams. New York: Oxford Uni-
    versity Press, 1973.

144 Davis, Angela. Angela Davis: An Autobiography.
    New York: Random House, 1974.

145 _____. If They Come in the Morning: Voices of
    Resistance. New York: Third Press, 1971.

146 Davis, R. California Women: A Guide to Their
    Politics, 1885-1911. San Francisco: California
    Scene, 1967.

147 Dawson, Richard, and Prewitt, Kenneth. Political
    Socialization: An Analytic Study. Boston: Little,
    Brown, 1969.

148 DeBeauvoir, Simone. The Second Sex. New York:
    Alfred A. Knopf, 1952.

149 Deckard, Barbara. The Women's Movement: Political,
    Socioeconomic and Psychological Issues. New York:
    Harper and Row, 1975.

150 DeCrow, Karen. The Young Woman's Guide to Libera-
    tion. New York: Pegasus, 1971.

151 Decter, Midge. The Liberated Woman and Other
    Americans. New York: Coward, McCann and Geog-
    hegan, 1971.

152 Degler, Carl N. Out of Our Past. New York: Harper
    and Row, 1958.

153 Delsman, Mary A. Everything You Need to Know About
    *ERA (*the Equal Rights Amendment). Riverside,
    Calif.: Meranza Press, 1975.

154 Domhoff, G. William. The Higher Circles: The
    Governing Class in America. New York: Random
    House, 1970.

155 _____. Who Rules America? Englewood Cliffs,
    N.J.: Prentice-Hall, 1967.

156 Donovan, Frank R. The Women in Their Lives: The

Distaff Side of the Founding Fathers. New York:
Dodd, Mead, 1966.

157 Douglas, Emily Taft. Remember the Ladies: The
Story of Great Women Who Helped Shape America.
New York: G. P. Putnam, 1966.

158 Dreyer, Edward and Rosenbaum, Walter A., eds.
Political Opinion and Behavior: Essays and
Studies. 2d ed. Belmont, Calif.: Wadsworth,
1970.

159 Drier, Mary. Margaret Drier Robins: Her Life,
Letters, and Work. New York: Island Press Co-
operative, 1950.

160 Drinnon, Richard. Rebel in Paradise: A Biography
of Emma Goldman. Chicago: University of Chicago
Press, 1961.

161 Drury, Allen. A Senate Journal: 1943-1945. New
York: McGraw-Hill, 1963.

162 Dunlap, Mary C. "The Equal Rights Amendment
and the Courts." See entry no. 680a.

163 Duster, Alfreda M., ed. Crusade for Justice: The
Autobiography of Ida B. Wells. Chicago: University
of Chicago Press, 1970.

164 Duverger, Maurice. The Political Role of Women.
Paris: UNESCO, 1955.

165 Easton, David, and Dennis, Jack. Children in the
Political System: Origins of Political Legitimacy.
New York: McGraw-Hill, 1969.

166 Ellman, Mary. Thinking About Women. New York:
Harcourt, Brace and World, 1968.

167 Engelbarts, Rudolf. Women in the United States Congress: 1917-1972. Littleton, Calif.: Libraries
Unlimited, 1974.

168 Engle, Paul. Women in the American Revolution.
Chicago: Follett, 1976.

169 Epstein, Cynthia Fuchs, and Goode, William J.,

eds. The Other Half: Roads to Women's
Equality. Englewood Cliffs, N.J.: Prentice-Hall,
1971.

170 Epstein, Laurily Keir, ed. Women in the Professions.
Lexington, Mass.: D.C. Heath, Lexington Books,
1975.

171 Faber, Doris. The Mothers of American Presidents.
New York: New American Library, 1968.

172 _____. Petticoat Politics: How American Women
Won the Right to Vote. New York: Lothrop, Lee
and Shephard, 1967.

173 Fairchild, Johnson E. Women, Society and Sex. New
York: Sheridan House, 1952.

174 Falk, Ruth; Maraventano, Frances; and Ralph, Diane.
A Woman's Place, An Updating of Women's Liberation. Washington, D.C.: National Institute of
Mental Health, Office of Youth and Study Affairs,
1970.

175 Farber, Seymour M., and Wilson, Roger H. L., eds.
Man and Civilization: The Potential of Women--
A Symposium. New York: McGraw-Hill, 1963.

176 Feldman, Sylvia. The Rights of Women. Rochelle
Park, N.J.: Hayden American Values Series, 1974.

177 Ferriss, Abbott. Indicators of Trends in the Status of
American Women. New York: Russell Sage Foundation, 1971.

178 Filene, Peter. Him/Her/Self: Sex Roles in Modern
America. New York: Harcourt Brace Jovanovich,
1975.

179 Firestone, Shulamith. The Dialectic of Sex: The Case
for Feminist Revolution. New York: William Morrow, 1970.

180 _____, and Koedt, Anne, eds. Notes From the
Second Year: Women's Liberation. New York:
Radical Feminists, 1970.

181 Fleming, Alice M. The Senator from Maine: Margaret
     Chase Smith. New York: Thomas Y. Crowell,
     1969.

182 Flexner, Eleanor. Century of Struggle: The Women's
     Rights Movement in the United States. Cambridge,
     Mass.: Harvard University Press, Belknap Press,
     1959.

183 Flynn, Elizabeth Gurley. Alderson Story: My Life as
     a Political Prisoner. New York: International,
     1972.

184 _____ . I Speak My Own Piece: Autobiography of
     'The Rebel Girl'. New York: Masses and Main-
     stream, 1955.

185 Fort Wayne, Indiana, Mayor's Commission on the
     Status of Women. Fort Wayne Women 1973-1974.
     1974.

186 Foster, G. Votes for Women. New York: Criterion,
     1966.

187 Frazier, Thomas R., ed. The Underside of American
     History: Other Readings, vol 2. New York: Har-
     court Brace Jovanovich, 1971.

188 Frederick, Pauline. Ten First Ladies of the World.
     New York: Meredith Press, 1967.

189 Frederikson, Carmen D. The Impact of Women
     Leaders of Davis County on a Changing Order.
     Logan, Utah: Agricultural Experiment Station,
     March 1959.

190 Freeman, Jo. The Politics of Women's Liberation.
     New York: David McKay, 1975.

191 _____ , ed. Women: A Feminist Perspective.
     Palo Alto, Calif.: Mayfield, 1975.

192 Friedan, Betty. The Feminine Mystique. New York:
     W. W. Norton, 1963.

193 _____ . It Changed My Life: Writings on the
     Women's Movement. New York: Random House,
     1976.

194 Friedman, Jean E., and Shade, William G. Our
     American Sisters: Women in American Life and
     Thought. Boston: Allyn and Bacon, 1973.

195 Gager, Nancy, ed. Women's Rights Almanac 1974.
     Bethesda, Md.: Elizabeth Cady Stanton, 1974.

196 Gallaher, Art, Jr. Plainville: Fifteen Years Later.
     New York: Columbia University Press, 1964.

197 Gans, Herbert J. The Levittowners. New York:
     Pantheon, 1967.

198 _____. The Urban Villagers. Glencoe, Ill.: Free
     Press, 1962.

199 Garskof, Michele, ed. Roles Women Play: Readings
     Toward Women's Liberation. Belmont, Calif.:
     Brooks, Cole, 1971.

200 Gattey, Charles N. The Bloomer Girls. New York:
     Coward-McCann, 1967.

201 General Federation of Women's Clubs. Women in High
     Level Positions. Washington, D.C.: Author, 1954.

202 Gibbs, Margaret. The DAR. New York: Holt, 1969.

203 Gildersleeve, Virginia. Many a Good Crusade. New
     York: Macmillan, 1954.

204 Glaser, William A., and Sills, David L., eds. The
     Government of Associations: Selections from the
     Behavioral Sciences. Totowa, N.J.: Bedminster
     Press, 1966.

205 Goldmark, Josephine. Impatient Crusader: Florence
     Kelley's Life Story. Urbana, Ill.: University of
     Illinois Press, 1953.

206 Good, Josephine. The History of Women in Republican
     Conventions and Women in the Republican National
     Committee. Washington, D.C.: Republican National
     Committee, Women's Division, April 1963.

207 Goot, Murray, and Reid, Elizabeth. Women and Voting
     Studies: Mindless Matrons or Sexist Scientism?
     Beverly Hills, Calif.: Sage, 1975.

208   Gornick, Vivian, and Moran, Barbara, eds. Women
      in Sexist Society: Studies in Power and Powerless-
      ness. New York: Basic Books, 1971.

209   Gouldner, Alvin W. Studies in Leadership: Leadership
      and Democratic Action. New York: Harper, 1950.

210   Graham, Frank. Margaret Chase Smith: Woman of
      Courage. New York: John Day, 1964.

211   Green, A. W. Recreation, Leisure and Politics. New
      York: McGraw-Hill, 1964.

212   Green, Constance. Washington: Capital City: 1879-
      1950. Princeton, N.J.: Princeton University Press,
      1963.

213   Greenstein, Fred I. Children and Politics. New
      Haven, Conn.: Yale University Press, 1965.

214   Greer, Dean William. The Application of Herbert
      Simon's Theory of Analyzing Social Movements to
      Women's Liberation. Boulder, Colo.: Educational
      Resources Information Center (ERIC), 1973.

215   Greer, Germaine. The Female Eunuch. New York:
      McGraw-Hill, 1971.

216   Grimes, Alan P. The Puritan Ethic and Woman Suf-
      frage. New York: Oxford University Press, 1967.

217   Grimstad, Kirsten, and Rennie, Susan, eds. The New
      Woman's Survival Catalogue. New York: Coward
      McCann and Geohegan, Berkeley Publishing, 1974.

218   _____, _____, eds. The New Woman's Survival
      Sourcebook. New York: Alfred A. Knopf, 1975.

219   Gross, Neal, and Trask, Anne E. The Sex Factor and
      the Management of Schools. New York: John Wiley,
      1976.

220   Gruberg, Martin. Women in Politics: An Assessment
      and Sourcebook. Oshkosh, Wis.: Academia Press,
      1968.

221   Gusfield, Joseph R. Symbolic Crusade: Status Politics

and the American Temperance Movement. Urbana,
Ill.: University of Illinois, 1963.

222   Hague, John A., ed. American Character and Culture.
Deland, Fla.: Everett-Edwards, 1964.

223   Hall, Florence Howe. Julia Ward Howe and the
Woman Suffrage Movement. New York: Arno Press,
1969.

224   Hall, Gus. Working Class Approach to Women's Liberation. New York: New Outlook, 1970.

225   Harbeson, Gladys E. Choice and Challenge for the
American Woman. Cambridge, Mass.: Schenkman,
1967.

226   Hareven, Tamara. Eleanor Roosevelt: An American
Conscience. New York: Quadrangle Books, 1968.

227   Harris, Louis. Is There a Republican Majority?
New York: Harper, 1954.

228   Harrison, Cynthia Ellen. Women's Movement Media:
A Source Guide. New York: R. R. Bowker,
1975.

229   Hatch, Alden. Ambassador Extraordinary: Claire
Boothe Luce. New York: Henry Holt, 1956.

230   Hausknecht, Murray. The Joiners: A Sociological
Description of Voluntary Association Membership in
the United States. Totowa, N.J.: Bedminster
Press, 1962.

231   Hays, Elinor Rice. Morning Star: A Biography of
Lucy Stone, 1818-1893. New York: Harcourt,
Brace and World, 1961.

232   Hecht, Marie B., et al., eds. The Women, Yes!
New York: Holt, Rinehart and Winston, 1973.

233   Hess, Robert D., and Torney, Judith V. The Development of Political Attitudes in Children. Chicago:
Aldine Press, 1967.

234   Hickok, Lorena A. Reluctant First Lady. New York:
Dodd, 1962.

235 Hicks, Nancy. The Honorable Shirley Chisholm:
     Congresswoman from Brooklyn. New York: Lion
     Press, 1971.

236 Holcomb, Morrigene. Women in the United States
     Congress. Rev. Washington, D.C.: Library of
     Congress, Congressional Research Service, 1975.

237 Hole, Judith, and Levine, Ellen. Rebirth of Feminism.
     New York: Quadrangle, 1971.

238 Holt, Rackham. Mary McLeod Bethune: A Biography.
     New York: Doubleday, 1964.

239 Horney, Karen. Feminine Psychology. New York:
     Norton, 1967.

240 Huber, Joan. Changing Woman in a Changing Society.
     Chicago: University of Chicago Press, 1973.

241 Hutcheson, John D., Jr., and Shevin, Jann. Citizen
     Groups in Local Politics: A Bibliographic Review.
     Santa Barbara, Calif.: Clio Books, 1976.

242 Hyman, Herbert. Political Socialization. Glencoe,
     Ill.: Free Press, 1959.

243 Iglitzin, Lynne B., and Ross, Ruth, eds. Women in
     the World: A Comparative Study. Santa Barbara,
     Calif.: Clio Books, 1976.

244 Indianapolis, Mayor's Task Force on Women, Commit-
     tee on Women in Government and Politics. Final
     Report. 1974.

245 Inter-American Commission of Women. Historical Re-
     view on the Recognition of the Political Rights of
     American Women. Washington: Pan American
     Union, 1965.

246 Irvine-Rivera, E. M. The Dry Blockade. Philadel-
     phia: Dorrance, 1951.

247 James, Bessie Rowland. Anne Royall's U.S.A. New
     Brunswick, N.J.: Rutgers University Press, 1972.

248 Janeway, Elizabeth. Between Myth and Morning:

Women Awakening. New York: William Morrow, 1974.

249 _____. Man's World, Woman's Place: A Study in Social Mythology. New York: William Morrow, 1971.

250 Janowitz, Morris, and Marvick, Dwaine. Competition, Pressure and Democratic Consent. Ann Arbor, Mich.: University of Michigan, Institute of Public Administration, Bureau of Government, 1956.

251 Jaquette, Jane S., ed. Women in Politics. New York: John Wiley, 1974.

252 Jenness, Linda, ed. Feminism and Socialism. New York: Pathfinder Press, 1972.

253 Jennings, M. Kent, and Niemi, Richard G. The Political Character of Adolescence: The Influence of Families and Schools. Princeton, N.J.: Princeton University Press, 1974.

254 Jensen, Oliver. The Revolt of American Women. New York: Harcourt Brace, 1952.

255 Johnson, Jalmer. Builders of the Northwest. New York: Dodd, Mead, 1963.

256 Johnson, Marilyn, and Stanwick, Kathy. Profile of Women Holding Office. Re-printed from Women in Public Office: A Biographical Directory and Statistical Analysis, compiled by Center for the American Woman and Politics. New York: R. R. Bowker, 1976. (Order reprint from Center for the American Woman and Politics, Rutgers University, New Brunswick, N.J., 08901, $3.00.)

257 Johnston, Johanna. Mrs. Satan: The Incredible Saga of Victoria C. Woodhull. New York: G. P. Putnam, 1967.

258 Joint Center for Political Studies. National Roster of Black Elected Officials, Volume 6. Washington, D.C.: Joint Center for Political Studies, 1976.

259 Jones, Katherine M. Heroines of Dixie: Confederate

Women Tell Their Story of the War. Indianapolis: Bobbs-Merrill, 1955.

260 Josephson, Hannah. Jeannette Rankin: First Lady in Congress. Indianapolis: Bobbs-Merrill, 1974.

261 Kanowitz, Leo. Women and the Law: The Unfinished Revolution. Albuquerque: University of New Mexico Press, 1971.

262 Katz, Elihu, and Lazarsfeld, Paul F. Personal Influence. Glencoe, Ill.: Free Press, 1955.

263 Katzenstern, Caroline. Lifting the Curtain: The State and National Woman Suffrage Campaigns in Pennsylvania as I Saw Them. Philadelphia: Dorrance, 1955.

264 Kayden, Xandra. The Handbook for Women Entering Politics. Cambridge, Mass.: Women Involved, Inc., 1973.

265 Kearney, James R. Anna Eleanor Roosevelt: The Evolution of a Reformer. Boston: Houghton Mifflin, 1968.

266 Kellen, Konrad. The Coming Age of Woman Power. New York: Peter H. Wyden, 1972.

267 Key, V. O., Jr. American State Politics. New York: Alfred A. Knopf, 1956.

268 _____. Politics, Parties, and Pressure Groups. 5th ed. New York: Thomas Y. Crowell, 1964.

269 Kirk, Russell. The Intelligent Woman's Guide to Conservatism. New York: Devin-Adair, 1957.

270 Kirkpatrick, Jeane. The New Presidential Elite: Men and Women in National Politics. New York: Russell Sage Foundation, 1976.

271 _____. Political Woman. New York: Basic Books, 1974.

272 Klagsburn, Francine, ed. The First Ms. Reader. New York: Ms. Magazine, 1973.

273 Klein, Viola. The Feminine Character: History of an
     Ideology. Urbana: University of Illinois, 1971.

274 Koedt, Anne; Levine, Ellen; and Rapone, Anita, eds.
     Radical Feminism. New York: Quadrangle, 1973.

275 Komarovsky, Mirra. Blue-Collar Marriage. New
     York: Random House, Vintage, 1967.

276 _____. Women in the Modern World: Their Educa-
     tion and Their Dilemmas. Boston: Little, Brown,
     1953.

277 Komisar, Lucy. The New Feminism. New York:
     Franklin Watts, 1971.

278 Kraditor, Aileen. The Ideas of the Woman Suffrage
     Movement, 1890-1920. New York: Columbia Uni-
     versity Press, 1965.

279 _____, ed. Up from the Pedestal: Selected
     Writings in History of American Feminism. Chi-
     cago: Quadrangle, 1970.

280 Kruschke, Earl R. The Woman Voter: An Analysis
     Based Upon Personal Interviews. Washington, D.C.:
     Public Affairs Press, 1955.

281 Kuriansky, Joan, and Smith, Catherine. Shirley
     Chisholm. Washington, D.C.: Grossman, 1972.

282 Ladner, Joyce A. Tomorrow's Tomorrow: The Black
     Woman. Garden City, N.Y.: Doubleday, 1971.

283 Lamson, Peggy. Few Are Chosen: American Women
     in Political Life Today. Boston: Houghton Mifflin,
     1968.

284 Lane, Robert E. Political Ideology. Glencoe, Ill.:
     Free Press, 1962.

285 _____. Political Life: Why People Get Involved in
     Politics. Glencoe, Ill.: Free Press, 1959.

286 Lasch, Christopher. The New Radicalism in America,
     1889-1963. New York: Alfred A. Knopf, 1965.

287 _____, ed. The Social Thought of Jane Addams.
Indianapolis: Bobbs-Merrill, 1965.

288 Lash, Joseph. Eleanor and Franklin. New York:
W. W. Norton, 1971.

289 _____. Eleanor: The Years Alone. New York:
W. W. Norton, 1972.

290 Lavin, Mildred H., and Oleson, Clara H., eds.
Women and Public Policy: A Humanistic Perspective. Iowa City, Iowa: University of Iowa, Institute of Public Affairs, 1974.

291 Lawson, Don. Frances Perkins, First Lady of the
Cabinet. London: Abelard-Schuman, 1966.

292 Lazarsfeld, Paul F.; Berelson, Bernard R.; and
Gaudet, Hazel. The People's Choice. New York:
Columbia University Press, 1968.

293 Leith, Priscilla M., ed. Politics Is for Women: All
You Need to Know About Being a Candidate, But
Were Afraid to Ask (Because You Are a Woman).
(Newton Women's Political Caucus, 335 Lake Ave.,
Newton Highlands, Mass., $1.95)

294 Lemmon, Melody Kay. The Unchanging Role of Women.
Boulder, Colo.: Educational Resources Information
Center (ERIC), 1974.

295 Lemons, James Stanley. The Woman Citizen: Social
Feminism in the 1920s. Urbana: University of
Illinois, 1973.

296 Lerner, Gerda. The Grimké Sisters from South
Carolina: Pioneers for Woman's Rights and Aboli-
tion. New York: Schocken Books, 1973.

297 _____. The Grimké Sisters from South Carolina:
Rebels Against Slavery. Boston: Houghton Mifflin,
1967.

298 _____. The Woman in American History. Reading,
Mass.: Addison-Wesley, 1971.

299 _____, ed. Black Women in White America: A

Documentary History. New York: Random House, 1972.

300 Levin, Murray B. The Alienated Voter. New York: Holt, Rinehart and Winston, 1960.

301 Levine, Daniel. Jane Addams and the Liberal Tradition. Madison, Wis.: State Historical Society of Wisconsin, 1971.

302 Levy, Richard G. Why Women Should Rule the World. New York: Vantage Press, 1952.

303 Lewis, William C. Declaration of Conscience. Garden City, N.Y.: Doubleday, 1972.

304 Lifton, Robert Jay, ed. The Woman in America. Boston: Beacon, 1964.

305 Lindzey, Gardner, and Aronson, Elliot. Handbook of Social Psychology, vol. 2, 2d ed. Reading, Mass.: Addison-Wesley, 1968.

306 Lipset, Seymour M. Political Man. Garden City, N.Y.: Doubleday, 1960.

307 Loeser, Herta. Women, Work, and Volunteering. Boston: Beacon Press, 1974.

308 Long, Priscilla, ed. The New Left: A Collection of Essays. Boston: Porter Sargent, 1969.

309 Lopata, Helena A. Occupation: Housewife. New York: Oxford University Press, 1971.

310 Loth, David. A Long Way Forward: The Biography of Congresswoman Frances P. Bolton. New York: Longmans, Green, 1957.

311 Louis Harris and Associates, Inc. The 1970 Virginia Slims American Women's Opinion Poll. New York: Louis Harris and Associates, Inc., 1970.

312 _____. The 1972 Virginia Slims American Women's Opinion Poll. New York: Louis Harris and Associates, Inc., 1972.

313 Lund, Caroline, and Stone, Betsey. <u>Women and the</u>
     <u>Equal Rights Amendment</u>. New York: Pathfinder
     Press, 1972.

314 Lutz, Alma. <u>Crusade for Freedom: Women of the</u>
     <u>Anti-Slavery Movement</u>. Boston: Beacon Press,
     1968.

315 _____. <u>Susan B. Anthony: Rebel, Crusader, Hu-</u>
     <u>manitarian</u>. Boston: Beacon Press, 1959.

316 Maccoby, Eleanor, ed. <u>The Development of Sex Dif-</u>
     <u>ferences</u>. Stanford, Calif.: Stanford University
     Press, 1966.

317 McGovern, Eleanor. <u>Uphill: A Personal Story</u>.
     Boston: Houghton Mifflin, 1974.

318 McGuigan, Dorothy, ed. <u>New Research on Women at</u>
     <u>the University of Michigan: Papers and Reports</u>.
     Ann Arbor, Mich.: University of Michigan, Center
     for the Continuing Education of Women, 1974.

319 _____, ed. <u>A Sampler of Women's Studies</u>. Ann
     Arbor, Mich.: University of Michigan, Center for
     Continuing Education of Women, 1973.

320 Macleod, Jennifer S., and Silverman, Sandra T. <u>'You</u>
     <u>Won't Do': What Textbooks on U.S. Government</u>
     <u>Teach High School Girls</u>. Pittsburgh: Know, 1973.

321 McPherson, Myra. <u>The Power Lovers: An Intimate</u>
     <u>Look at Politics and Marriage</u>. New York: G. P.
     Putnam, 1975.

322 Marberry, M. M. <u>Vicky: A Biography of Victoria</u>
     <u>C. Woodhull</u>. New York: Funk and Wagnalls, 1967.

323 Martin, Wendy, ed. <u>American Sisterhood: Writings</u>
     <u>of the Feminist Movement from Colonial Times to</u>
     <u>the Present</u>. New York: Harper and Row, 1972.

324 Martinez, Barbara Fully, and Weiner, Roberta. <u>The</u>
     <u>How-to Press and PR Handbook</u>. Washington, D.C.:
     National Women's Political Caucus.

325 Mead, Margaret, and Kaplan, Frances B., eds.

American Women: The Report of the President's
Commission on the Status of Women and Other
Publications of the Commission. New York:
Charles Scribner, 1965.

326 Means, Marianna. The Women in the White House:
The Lives, Times, and Influence of Twelve Notable
First Ladies. New York: Random House, 1963.

327 Meigs, Cornelia. Jane Addams: Pioneer for Social
Justice: A Biography. Boston: Little, Brown,
1970.

328 Merelman, Richard M. Political Socialization and
Educational Climates: A Study of Two School Districts. New York: Holt, Rinehart and Winston,
1971.

329 Merriam, Eve. After Nora Slammed the Door.
American Women in the 1960's: The Unfinished
Revolution. Cleveland, Ohio: World, 1964.

330 _____. Growing Up Female in America: Ten Lives.
Garden City, N.Y.: Doubleday, 1971.

331 Meyer, Agnes E. Out of These Roots: The Autobiography of an American Woman. Boston: Little,
Brown, 1953.

332 Milbrath, Lester. Political Participation. Chicago:
Rand-McNally, 1965.

333 Milburn, Josephine F. Women as Citizens: A Comparative Review. Beverly Hills, Calif.: Sage,
1976.

334 Miller, Helen Hill. Carrie Chapman Catt: The Power
of an Idea. Washington, D.C.: Carrie Chapman
Catt Memorial Fund, Inc., 1958.

335 Miller, Mary E. WOVEN - Women's Ohio Volunteer
Employment Network. Columbus, Ohio: Ohio State
University, Mershon Center, Women's Ohio Volun-
teer Employment Network, 1975.

336 Millett, Kate. Sexual Politics. Garden City, N.Y.:
Doubleday, 1970.

337   Millman, Marcia, and Kanter, Rosabeth Moss, eds.
      Another Voice: Feminist Perspectives on Social
      Life and Social Science. New York: Doubleday,
      Anchor, 1975.

338   Mitchell, Juliet. Woman's Estate. New York: Random
      House, Vintage Books, 1973.

339   Moffett, Toby. Nobody's Business: The Political In-
      truder's Guide to Everyone's State Legislature.
      Riverside, Conn.: Chatham Press, 1973.

340   Monsen, R. Joseph, Jr., and Cannon, Mark W. The
      Makers of Public Policy: American Power Groups
      and Their Ideologies. New York: McGraw-Hill,
      1965.

341   Montgomery, Ruth. Mrs. LBJ. New York: Holt,
      Rinehart, and Winston, 1964.

342   Morgan, David. Suffragists and Democrats: The Poli-
      tics of Woman Suffrage in America. East Lansing,
      Mich.: Michigan State University Press, 1972.

343   Morgan, Robin, ed. Sisterhood Is Powerful: An
      Anthology of Writings from the Women's Liberation
      Movement. New York: Random House, Vintage
      Books, 1970.

344   _____, ed. Women in Revolt. New York: Random
      House, 1969.

345   Murphy, Irene L. The Politics of Sex Discrimination:
      Optimal National Policy on the Status of Women for
      the Seventies. New Brunswick, N.J.: Rutgers
      University, Eagleton Institute of Politics, 1973.

346   _____. Public Policy on the Status of Women: An
      Agenda and Strategy for the Seventies. Lexington,
      Mass.: D. C. Heath, Lexington Books, 1973.

347   Myers, Elizabeth P. Madam Secretary: Frances
      Perkins. New York: Julian Messner, 1972.

348   Myrdal, Alva, and Klein, Viola. Women's Two Roles.
      New York: Humanities, 1968.

349   Nadelson, Regina. <u>Who Is Angela Davis?: The Biog-</u>
      <u>raphy of a Revolutionary.</u> New York: Peter H.
      Wyden, 1972.

350   National Commission on the Observance of International
      Women's Year. <u>".. . To Form a More Perfect</u>
      <u>Union. . ." Justice for American Women.</u> Washing-
      ton, D.C.: U.S. Government Printing Office, 1976.

351   National Conference on Women in Educational Policy
      Making. National Conference on Women in Educa-
      tion. <u>Hierarchy, Power, and Women in Education</u>
      <u>Policy Making.</u> IEL Reports: Six. Washington,
      D.C.: Institute for Educational Leadership, George
      Washington University, 1976.

352   _____. _____. <u>Women in Educational Leadership:</u>
      <u>An Open Letter to State Legislators.</u> IEL Reports:
      Four. Washington, D.C.: Institute for Educational
      Leadership, George Washington University, 1976.

353   National League of Cities. <u>Women in Municipal Govern-</u>
      <u>ment.</u> Washington, D.C.: National League of Cities,
      1974.

354   National Organization for Women. Task Force on
      Women and Volunteerism. <u>Volunteer Beware: Guide-</u>
      <u>lines for Discussion.</u> Chicago: National Organiza-
      tion for Women (NOW), 1973.

355   _____. _____. <u>Volunteer--Why Not? Analysis</u>
      <u>and Answers.</u> Chicago: National Organization for
      Women (NOW), 1973.

356   _____. _____. <u>Volunteerism: What It's All</u>
      <u>About.</u> Chicago: National Organization for Women
      (NOW), 1973.

357   National School Boards Association. <u>Women on School</u>
      <u>Boards.</u> Evanston, Ill.: National School Boards
      Association, 1974.

358   National Women's Education Fund. <u>Campaign Techniques</u>
      <u>Workshop.</u> Milwaukee, Wis.: Alverno College, 1974.

359   National Women's Political Caucus. <u>Catalogue for Politi-</u>
      <u>cal Women.</u> Washington, D.C.: National Women's
      Political Caucus.

360 _____. Preliminary Steps in a Political Campaign.
Washington, D.C.: National Women's Political
Caucus.

361 Nestor, Agnes. Woman's Labor Leader: The Autobiography of Agnes Nestor. Rockford, Ill.: Belle-
vue, 1954.

362 Neuberger, Richard L. Adventures in Politics. New
York: Oxford University Press, 1954.

363 New Jersey School Boards Association. Number and
Percent of Women Board Members in New Jersey
by County, 1974-1975. Trenton, N.J.: New Jersey
School Boards Association.

364 Newland, Kathleen. Women in Politics: A Global Review. Worldwatch Paper 3. Washington, D.C.:
Worldwatch Institute, December 1975.

365 New York (City). Commission on Human Rights.
Women's Role in Contemporary Society. Edited by
Elizabeth Norton. New York: Avon, 1972.

366 New York (State). Governor's Committee on the Education and Employment of Women. New York Women
and Their Changing World. Albany, N.Y.: State of
New York, 1964.

367 Nies, Judith. Message to the Future: The Tradition
of Radical Women in America. New York: Holt,
Rinehart and Winston, 1974.

368 Noun, Louise R. Strong-Minded Women: The Emergence of the Woman-Suffrage Movement in Iowa.
Ames, Iowa: Iowa State University Press, 1969.

369 Oakley, Violet. Cathedral of Compassion: Dramatic
Outline of the Life of Jane Addams, 1860-1935.
Philadelphia: Women's International League for
Peace and Freedom, 1955.

370 Odegard, Peter H., and Baerwald, Hans H. The
American Republic: Its Government and Politics.
New York: Harper and Row, 1964.

371 O'Neill, William L. Everyone Was Brave: A History

of Feminism in America.   Chicago: Quadrangle, 1971.

372 _____. Everyone Was Brave: The Rise and Fall of Feminism in America.   Chicago: Quadrangle, 1969.

373 _____, ed.   The Woman's Movement: Feminism in the United States and England.   Chicago: Quadrangle, 1971.

374 Pannell, Anne Gary, and Wyatt, Dorothea E.   Julia S. Tutwiler and Social Progress in Alabama.   Auburn, Ala.: University of Alabama Press, 1961.

375 Park, Maud.   Front Door Lobby.   Edited by Edna L. Stantial.   Boston: Beacon Press, 1960.

376 Pateman, Carole.   Participation and Democratic Theory. New York: Cambridge University Press, 1970.

377 Pauli, Hertha.   Her Name Was Sojourner Truth.   New York: Avon Books, 1972.

378 Paulson, Ross E.   Women's Suffrage and Prohibition: A Comparative Study of Equality and Social Control. Glenview, Illinois: Scott, Foresman, 1973.

379 Pellet, Betty, with Klein, Alexander.   That Pellet Woman! New York: Stein and Day, 1965.

380 Perry, Robert T.   Black Legislators.   San Francisco: R and E Research Associates, 1976.

381 Peters, Barbara, and Samuels, Victoria, eds.   Dialogue on Diversity: A New Agenda for American Women.   1976. (Institute on Pluralism and Group Identity, 165 East 56 Street, New York, N.Y. 10022)

382 Phillips, Ruth, ed.   Forty Years of a Great Idea. Washington, D.C.:   League of Women Voters, 1960.

383 Pomper, Gerald.   Voters' Choice: Varieties of American Electoral Behavior.   New York: Dodd, Mead, 1975.

384 Proxmire, Ellen.   One Foot in Washington: The Perilous Life of a Senator's Wife.   Washington, D.C.: Robert B. Luce, 1963.

385 Putnam, Emily James. The Lady: Studies of Certain Significant Phases of Her History. Chicago: University of Chicago, 1969.

386 Rainwater, Lee; Coleman, Richard P.; and Handel, Gerald. Workingman's Wife: Her Personality, World and Life Style. New York: Oceana, 1959.

387 Ralph Nader Congress Project. Citizens Look at Congress. Bella S. Abzug, Democratic Representative from New York. Washington, D.C.: Grossman, 1972.

388 _____ . _____ . Edith Green, Democratic Representative from Oregon. Washington, D.C.: Grossman, 1972.

389 _____ . _____ . Ella T. Grasso, Democratic Representative from Connecticut. Washington, D.C.: Grossman, 1972.

390 _____ . _____ . Julia Butler Hansen, Democratic Representative from Washington. Washington, D.C.: Grossman, 1972.

391 _____ . _____ . Leonor K. Sullivan, Democratic Representative from Missouri. Washington, D.C.: Grossman, 1972.

392 _____ . _____ . Louise Day Hicks, Democratic Representative from Massachusetts. Washington, D.C.: Grossman, 1972.

393 _____ . _____ . Margaret M. Heckler, Republican Representative from Massachusetts. Washington, D.C.: Grossman, 1972.

394 _____ . _____ . Patsy T. Mink, Democratic Representative from Hawaii. Washington, D.C.: Grossman, 1972.

395 Reed, Evelyn. Problems of Women's Liberation: A Marxist Approach. New York: Pathfinder, 1971.

396 Reeves, Nancy. Womankind: Beyond the Stereotypes. Chicago: Aldine-Atherton, 1971.

397 Reid, Inez. "Together" Black Women. New York:
     Emerson Hall, 1972.

398 Reische, Diana L. , ed. Women and Society. New
     York: H. W. Wilson, 1972.

399 Republican National Committee. Women's Division.
     The History of Women in the Republican National
     Conventions and Women in the Republican National
     Committee. Washington, D.C.: Republican National
     Committee, Women's Division, 1963.

400 _____. _____. Women in Public Service. Wash-
     ington, D.C.: Republican National Committee,
     Women's Division, 1972.

401 Revel, Jean-François. Without Marx or Jesus: The
     New American Revolution Has Begun. Garden City,
     N.Y.: Doubleday, 1971.

402 Riegal, Robert E. American Feminists. Lawrence,
     Kans.: University of Kansas Press, 1963.

403 _____. American Women: A Story of Social Change.
     Teaneck, N.J.: Fairleigh Dickinson University
     Press, 1970.

404 Riley, Matilda White, and Foner, Anne. An Inventory
     of Research Findings. Aging and Society, vol. 1.
     New York: Russell Sage Foundation, 1968.

405 Roberts, Joan I. Women Scholars on Woman. New
     York: David McKay, 1976.

406 Robinson, Wilhelmena S. Historical Negro Biographies.
     Las Vegas, Nev.: Publishers, 1968.

407 Roosevelt, Eleanor. Autobiography. New York: Harper,
     1961.

408 _____. Tomorrow Is Now. New York: Harper, 1963.

409 _____, and Hickok, Lorena A. Ladies of Courage.
     New York: Putnam, 1954.

410 Roper Organization, Inc. The Virginia Slims American
     Women's Opinion Poll, volume 3. Williamstown,
     Mass.: The Roper Organization, Inc., 1974.

411   Rosaldo, Michelle, and Lamphere, Louise, eds.
      Woman, Culture and Society. Stanford, Calif.:
      Stanford University Press, 1974.

412   Rose, Arnold. The Power Structure: Political Process
      in American Society. New York: Oxford University
      Press, 1967.

413   Rosenau, James N. Citizenship Between Elections.
      New York: Free Press, 1974.

414   Ross, Ishbel. The President's Wife: Mary Todd
      Lincoln. New York: G. P. Putnam, 1973.

415   Ross, Susan C. The Rights of Women: The Basic
      ACLU Guide to a Woman's Rights. New York:
      Avon, Discus Books, 1973.

416   Rossi, Alice S., ed. The Feminist Papers: From
      Adams to De Beauvoir. New York: Columbia Uni-
      versity Press, 1973.

417   _____, and Calderwood, Ann, eds. Academic Women
      on the Move. New York: Russell Sage Foundation,
      1973.

418   Roszak, Betty, and Roszak, Theodore. Masculine/
      Feminine: Readings in the Sexual Mythology and the
      Liberation. New York: Harper and Row, 1969.

419   Ryan, Mary P. Womanhood in America: From
      Colonial Times to the Present. New York: New
      Viewpoints, 1975.

420   Safilios-Rothschild, Constantina. Women and Social
      Policy. Englewood Cliffs, N. J.: Prentice-Hall,
      1974.

421   _____, ed. Toward a Sociology of Women. Lexing-
      ton, Mass.: Xerox College, 1972.

422   Salper, Roberta, ed. Female Liberation: History and
      Current Politics. New York: Alfred A. Knopf, 1972.

423   Samuels, Catherine. The Forgotten Five Million:
      Women in Public Employment. A Guide to Elimina-
      ting Sex Discrimination. New York: Women's Action
      Alliance, 1975.

424 Sanders, Marion K. The Lady and the Vote. Boston:
     Houghton Mifflin, 1956.

425 Sargent, Lyman T., ed. New Left Thought: An Intro-
     duction. Homewood, Ill.: Dorsey Press, 1972.

426 Schlesinger, James A. Ambition and Politics: Politi-
     cal Careers in the U.S. Chicago: Rand McNally,
     1966.

427 Schneir, Miriam, ed. Feminism: The Essential His-
     torical Writings. New York: Random House, 1972.

428 Scott, Ann, and Komisar, Lucy. ... And Justice For
     All: Federal Equal Opportunity Enforcement Effort
     Against Sex Discrimination. Chicago: National
     Organization for Women (NOW), 1971.

429 Scott, Anne Firor. The Southern Lady: From Pede-
     stal to Politics, 1830-1930. Chicago: University
     of Chicago Press, 1970.

430 _____, ed. The American Woman: Who Was She?
     Englewood Cliffs, N.J.: Prentice-Hall, 1971.

431 _____, ed. What Is Happening to American Women.
     Atlanta, Ga.: Southern Newspaper Publishers Asso-
     ciation Foundation Seminar Books, 1970.

432 _____ and Scott, Andrew M. One Half the People:
     The Fight for Woman Suffrage. Philadelphia: J. B.
     Lippincott, 1975.

433 Seay, Ruth, ed. The Continuum Center for Women:
     Education, Volunteerism, Employment. Battle
     Creek, Michigan: W. K. Kellogg Foundation, 1973.

434 Seifer, Nancy. Nobody Speaks for Me!: Self-Portraits
     of American Working Class Women. New York:
     Simon and Schuster, 1976.

435 Severn, Williams. Free But Not Equal: How Women
     Won the Right to Vote. New York: Julian Messner,
     1967.

436 Shadegg, Stephen C. Clare Boothe Luce. New York:
     Simon and Schuster, 1970.

437   Shaw, George Bernard. The Intelligent Woman's Guide
       to Socialism, Capitalism, Sovietism and Facism.
       New York: Vintage, 1972.

438   Siddon, Sally Goodyear. Consider Yourself for Public
       Office. Washington, D. C.: National Federation of
       Republican Women, 1976.

439   Sinclair, Andrew. The Better Half: The Emancipation
       of the American Woman. New York: Harper and
       Row, 1965.

440   Smith, Constance, and Freedman, Anne. Voluntary
       Associations: Perspectives on the Literature.
       Cambridge, Mass.: Harvard University Press,
       1972.

441   Smith, Margaret Chase. Declaration of Conscience.
       Garden City, N. Y.: Doubleday, 1972.

442   _____, and Jeffers, H. Paul. Gallant Women. New
       York: McGraw-Hill, 1968.

443   Smith, Page. Daughters of the Promised Land: Women
       in American History. Boston: Little, Brown, 1970.

444   Smuts, Robert. Women and Work in America. New
       York: Columbia University Press, 1959.

445   Snyder, Charles McCool. Dr. Mary Walker, Little
       Lady in Pants. New York: Vantage Press, 1962.

446   Sochen, June. Herstory: A Woman's View of American
       History. New York: Alfred A. Knopf, 1974.

447   _____. Movers and Shakers: American Women
       Thinkers and Activists, 1900-1970. New York:
       Quadrangle Books, 1973.

448/9 _____, ed. The New Feminism in Twentieth Century
       America. Lexington, Mass.: D. C. Heath, 1971.

450   Southern Methodist University. The Education of Women
       for Social and Political Leadership. Dallas, Tex.:
       Southern Methodist University Press, 1967.

451   Stern, Madeleine B. Purple Passage: The Life of

Mrs. Frank Leslie. Norman, Okla.: University of
Oklahoma Press, 1953.

452   Stevenson, Janet. Women's Rights. New York: Watts,
1972.

453   Stimpson, Catharine R., ed. Discrimination Against
Women. New York: R. R. Bowker, 1973.

454   Stinson, Thomas. Voluntary Labor and Non-Metropoli-
tan Local Government. Washington, D.C.: U.S.
Economic Research Service, 1970.

455   Stoddard, Hope. Famous American Women. New
York: Thomas Y. Crowell, 1970.

456   Stouffer, Samuel. Communism, Conformity and Civil
Liberties: A Cross-Section of the Nation Speaks Its
Mind. Garden City, N.Y.: Doubleday, 1955.

457   Stowe, Lyman Beecher. Saints, Sinners, and Beechers.
Freeport, N.Y.: Books for Libraries Press, 1970.

458   Strauss, A. L. League of Women Voters. Washington,
D.C.: League of Women Voters, 1950.

459   Strayer, Martha. The D.A.R.: An Informal History.
Washington, D.C.: Public Affairs Press, 1958.

460   A Study of the League of Women Voters of the United
States. 5 vols. Ann Arbor: University of Michigan,
Institute for Social Research, Survey Research Center,
1956-1958.

461   Suhl, Yuri. Ernestine Rose and the Battle for Human
Rights. New York: Reynal, 1959.

462   Sullerot, Evelyne. Woman, Society and Change. New
York: McGraw-Hill, 1971.

463   Sullivan, Denis G., et al. The Politics of Representation: The Democratic Convention 1972. New York:
St. Martin's Press, 1974.

464   Sussman, Marvin B., ed. Community Structure and
Analysis. New York: Thomas Y. Crowell, 1959.

465 Tait, Marjorie. The Education of Women for Citizen-
     ship: Some Practical Suggestions. Basle: UNESCO,
     1954.

466 Talmadge, John Erwin. Rebecca Latimer Felton:
     Nine Stormy Decades. Athens, Ga.: University of
     Georgia Press, 1960.

467 Tanner, Leslie B., ed. Voices from Women's Libera-
     tion. New York: Signet, 1970.

468 Taylor, Antoinette Elizabeth. The Woman Suffrage
     Movement in Tennessee. New York: Bookman,
     1957.

469 Thompson, Mary Lou, ed. Voices of the New Femi-
     nism. Boston: Beacon Press, 1970.

470 Tims, Margaret. Jane Addams of Hull House, 1860-
     1935: A Centenary Study. New York: Macmillan,
     1961.

471 Tingsten, Herbert. Political Behavior. Totowa, N. J.:
     Bedminster Press, 1963.

472 Tinker, Irene, and Bramsen, Michele, eds. Women
     and World Development. Washington, D. C.: Over-
     seas Development Council, 1976.

473 Tolchin, Susan. Women in Congress: 1917-1976.
     Washington, D. C.: U. S. Government Printing Office,
     1976.

474 _____, and Tolchin, Martin. Clout: Womanpower
     and Politics. New York: Coward, McCann, and
     Geoghegan, 1974.

475 Tomalin, Claire. The Life and Death of Mary Woll-
     stonecraft. New York: Harcourt Brace Jovanovich,
     1974.

476 Tripp, Maggie. Woman in the Year 2000. New York:
     Arbor House, 1974.

477 United Nations. Commission on the Status of Women.
     Constitutions, Electoral Laws and Other Legal Instru-
     ments Relating to the Political Rights of Women.
     New York: United Nations Publications, 1968.

478 _____ . Department of Economic and Social Affairs.
Civic and Political Education of Women. New York:
United Nations Publications, 1971.

479 _____ . _____ . The Convention on the Political
Rights of Women: History and Commentary. New
York: United Nations Publications, 1956.

480 _____ . _____ . Political Education of Women:
Pamphlet Produced at the Request of the Commis-
sion on the Status of Women. New York: United
Nations Publications, 1951.

481 _____ . General Assembly. Political Rights of
Women: Report of the Secretary-General. New
York: United Nations Publications, December 1970.

482 United States. Civil Service Commission. Intergovern-
mental Personnel Programs. Women in State and
Local Governments: EEO for State and Local
Governments. Washington, D.C.: U.S. Civil
Service Commission, 1972.

483 _____ . Department of Commerce. Bureau of the
Census. A Statistical Portrait of Women in the
U.S. Washington, D.C.: U.S. Government Printing
Office, 1976.

484 _____ . Department of Labor. Women in the World
Today: Women in High Level Elective and Appointive
Positions in National Governments. Washington,
D.C : U.S. Department of Labor, 1963.

485 _____ . _____ . Manpower Administration.
Americans Volunteer, 1969. Washington, D.C.:
U.S. Government Printing Office, 1970.

486 _____ . _____ . _____ . Americans Volunteer,
1974. Washington, D.C.: U.S. Government Printing
Office, 1975.

487 _____ . _____ . Women's Bureau. 1969 Handbook
on Women Workers. Washington, D.C.: U.S.
Government Printing Office, 1969.

488 _____ . _____ . _____ . 1975 Handbook on
Women Workers. Washington, D.C.: U.S. Government Printing Office, 1975.

489 _____ . _____ . _____ . Report of a Conference
on Woman's Destiny, Choice or Chance? Washington,
D. C.: U. S. Government Printing Office, 1963.

490 _____ . _____ . _____ . The Status of Women
in the United States. Washington, D. C.: U. S.
Government Printing Office, 1953.

491 _____ . _____ . _____ . Women of the 80th -
90th Congress, 1946-67. Washington, D. C.: U. S.
Government Printing Office, 1967.

492 _____ . _____ . _____ . Women Serving in
State Legislatures. Washington, D. C.: U. S. Government Printing Office, 1952.

493 _____ . Department of State. Human Rights: Some
Next Steps. Washington, D. C.: U. S. Government
Printing Office, 1963.

494 _____ . Interdepartmental Committee on the Status of
Women. American Women 1963-1968. Washington,
D. C.: U. S. Government Printing Office, 1968.

495 _____ . President's Commission on the Status of
Women. American Women - Report of the President's
Commission on the Status of Women. Washington,
D. C.: U. S. Government Printing Office, 1963.

496 _____ . _____ . Committee on Civil and Political
Rights. Report of the Committee on Civil and Political Rights to the President's Commission on the
Status of Women. Washington, D. C.: U. S. Government Printing Office, 1964.

497 Van Helden, Morrigene. Freshman Women Members of
the 93rd Congress. Washington, D. C.: Library of
Congress, Congressional Research Service, 1973.

498 _____ . Women in the United States Congress.
Washington, D. C.: Library of Congress, Congressional Research Service, 1971.

499 Van Riper, Paul P. Handbook of Practical Politics.
2d ed. Evanston, Ill.: Row, Peterson, 1950.

500 Verba, Sidney, and Nie, Norman H. Participation in

America: Political Democracy and Social Equality.
New York: Harper and Row, 1972.

501 Wahlke, John C. et al. The Legislative System: Explorations in Legislative Behavior. New York: John Wiley, 1962.

502 Walker, Lola C. The Speeches and Speaking of Carrie Chapman Catt. Cambridge, Mass.: Harvard College Library, 1959.

503 Wallace, David. First Tuesday: A Study of Rationality in Voting. Garden City, N.Y.: Doubleday, 1964.

504 Ware, Cellestine. Woman Power: The Movement for Women's Liberation. New York: Tower Publications, 1970.

505 Watkins, Mel, and David, Jay, eds. Black Woman: Portraits in Fact and Fiction. New York: William Morrow, 1970.

506 Wells, Mildred White. Unity in Diversity: The History of the General Federation of Women's Clubs Since 1889. Washington, D.C.: General Federation of Women's Clubs, 1953.

507 Wertheimer, Barbara M., and Nelson, Anne H. Trade Union Women: A Study of Their Participation in New York City Locals. New York: Praeger, 1975.

508 White, Theodore H. The Making of the President, 1972. New York: Atheneum, 1973.

509 Whitton, Mary O. These Were the Women: U.S.A., 1776-1860. New York: Hastings House, 1954.

510 Williams, Clare B. The History of the Founding and Development of the National Federation of Republican Women. Washington, D.C.: Republican National Committee, Women's Division, fall 1962/spring 1963.

511 Williams, Maxine, and Newman, Pamela. Black Women's Liberation. New York: Pathfinder Press, 1972.

512 Williams, Robin, Jr. American Society: A Sociological

Interpretation. 3d ed. New York: Alfred A. Knopf, 1970.

513 Wilson, James Q. The Amateur Democrats: Club Politics in Three Cities. Chicago: University of Chicago Press, 1962.

514 Wise, Winifred. Rebel in Petticoats: The Life of Elizabeth Cady Stanton. Philadelphia: Chilton, 1960.

515 Wolff, Robert, ed. Styles of Political Action in America. New York: Random House, 1972.

516 Women's Incentives for Community Participation in Policy Issues. Kalamazoo: Western Michigan University, School of Social Work, Field Studies in Research and Practice, 1972.

517 Women's Research Center of Boston. Who Rules Massachusetts Women. Part I: State Government. Cambridge, Mass.: Women's Research Center of Boston, Center for the Study of Public Policy.

518 Woodward, Helen. The Lady Persuaders. Stamford, Conn.: Astor-Honor, 1960.

519 Wortis, Helen, and Rabinowitz, Clara, eds. The Women's Movement: Social and Psychological Perspectives. New York: Halsted, 1972.

520 Young, Louise. Understanding Politics: A Practical Guide for Women. New York: Pellegrini and Cudahy, 1950.

ARTICLES

521 Abernathy, Maureen H. "Women Judges in the United States Courts." Women Lawyers Journal 55 (spring 1969).

522 Abramowitz, S. I. "Would a Woman President Really Make a Difference?" Seventeen 31 (June 1972): 33.

523 Abzug, Bella S. "Our White, Male, Middle-Class, Middle-Aged Congress." AAUW Journal (November 1971): 33-34.

524 _____, and Edgar, Cynthia. "Women and Politics: The Struggle for Representation." Massachusetts Review 13 (winter/spring 1972): 17-24.

525 _____, et al. "Women in the Democratic Party: A Review of Affirmative Action." Columbia Human Rights Law Review 6 (spring 1974): 3-24.

526 Ade, Ginny. "The Making of a Woman President." Progressive Woman 2 (January 1972): 14-17.

527 _____. "One-Year Job: White House Fellow." Progressive Woman 2 (February 1972): 14.

528 Alexander, S. "Letter to the Founding Mother." Newsweek 80 (24 July 1972): 37.

529 Allen, Ethel D. "The Need for Women in Politics." In The Role of Women in Politics, edited by Mae R. Carter. Newark, Del.: University of Delaware, Division of Continuing Education, 1974.

530 Allen, Florence C. "Women in Public Office." Women Lawyers Journal 44 (summer 1958): 12.

531 Allen, G. "Party Girl." Ladies Home Journal 79 (November 1962): 68-69.

532   Allen, S. V. "It Wouldn't Have Happened Without Her:
      The Role of Governors' Wives." Compact 8 (July
      1974): 2-4.

533   "The American Woman." Time (20 March 1972): see
      entire issue.

534   "The American Woman: On the Move But Where?"
      U.S. News and World Report (8 December 1975):
      54-74.

535   Anderson, Jack. "President Nixon and the Women."
      Parade (31 October 1971): 4.

536   Anderson, Kristi. "Working Women and Political
      Participation, 1952-1972." American Journal of
      Political Science 19 (August 1975): 439-455.

537   Anderson, Lee Berger. "NAWL Driving for Ratifica-
      tion of Equal Rights Amendment." Women Lawyers
      Journal 59 (winter 1973): 3.

538   Angrist, S. S. "Role Constellation as a Variable in
      Women's Leisure Activities." Social Forces 45
      (March 1967): 423-431.

539   Arnott, Catherine. "Feminists and Anti-Feminists as
      'True Believers'." Sociology and Social Research
      57 (April 1973): 300-306.

540   Arnstein, W. L. "Votes for Women: Myths and
      Reality." History Today 18 (August 1968): 531-539.

541   "As Maine Goes...." Time 76 (5 September 1960):
      13-16.

542   Athey, Louis. "Florence Kelley and the Quest for
      Negro Equality." Journal of Negro History 56
      (October 1971): 249-261.

543   Babchuk, Nicholas, and Booth, Alan. "Voluntary Asso-
      ciation Membership: A Longitudinal Analysis."
      American Sociological Review 34 (February 1968):
      31-45.

544   _____; Marsey, Ruth; and Gordon, C. Wayne. "Men

and Women in Community Agencies: A Note on
Power and Prestige." American Sociological Review 25 (June 1960): 399-403.

545 Bardizh, O. "Women in the Class Struggle: A Review
of Some Books and Magazines." World Marxist Review 17 (March 1974): 130-133.

546 Barker, S. E. "You Never Know Until You Try:
Candidate for County Recorder." Independent Woman
30 (January 1951): 5.

547 Barth, Ilene. "Congresswoman Pat Schroeder: Politician and 'Troublemaker'." Ms. 4 (June 1976): 62.

548 _____. "Our Five New Congresswomen--How They
Got There, What They Hope to Do." Parade (25
February 1973): 13.

549 Batdorff, E. R. "Hard Work: She Likes It." Independent Woman 32 (December 1953): 441-442.

550 Baxandall, Rosalyn; Gordon, Linda; and Reverby, Susan.
"Boston Working Women Protest, 1869." Signs:
Journal of Women in Culture and Society 1 (spring
1976): 803-808.

551 Beeman, Alice, and McCune, Shirley. "Changing
Styles: Women's Groups in the 70's." AAUW
Journal 64 (November 1970): 24-26.

552 "Bella." Newsweek 76 (5 October 1970): 28-29.

553 "Bellacose Abzug." Time 98 (16 August 1971): 14.

554 Bellush, Jewel. "Books in Review: The Politicization
of American Women." National Civic Review
(September 1976): 420-430.

555 Bem, Sandra, and Bem, Daryl. "Case Study of Non-
conscious Ideology: Training the Woman to Know Her
Place." In Beliefs, Attitudes and Human Affairs,
edited by Daryl Bem. Belmont, Calif.: Brooks
Cole, 1970.

556 Bennett, Edward M., and Goodwin, Harriet M. "Emo-
tional Aspects of Political Behavior: The Woman

Voter." Genetic Psychology Monographs 58 (1958): 3-53.

557   Bennett, Stephen E., and Klecka, William R. "Social Status and Political Participation: A Multivariate Analysis of Predictive Power." Midwest Journal of Political Science 14 (August 1970): 355-382.

558   Benson, Lucy W. "Women Suffrage." National Civic Review 60 (May 1970): 252-255.

559   Bernstein, Robert A., and Pally, Jayne D. "Race, Class and Support for Female Candidates." Western Political Quarterly 28 (December 1975): 733-736.

560   Bertelsen, Judy. "Political Interest, Influence and Efficacy: Differences Between the Sexes and Among Marital Status Groups." American Political Quarterly 2 (October 1974): 412-426.

561   Bettelheim, Bruno. "Women: Emancipation Is Still to Come." New Republic 151 (7 November 1964): 48-58.

562   Bezdek, William, and Strodtbeck, Fred L. "Sex-Role Identity and Pragmatic Action." American Sociological Review 35 (June 1970): 491-502.

563   Bird, A. T. "Women in Politics - Changing Perceptions." Journal of the Association for the Study of Perception 10 (1975): 1-9.

564   Bird, Caroline. "The Case for a Female President." New Woman (April/May 1972): 32-35.

565   _____. "Out to Finish What the Suffragettes Started." Think (publication of IBM) (July/August 1970).

566   _____. "Women Who Make Great Success Have Husbands Who Make Coffee." New Woman 1 (November 1971): 64.

567   "Black Lawmakers in Congress." Ebony 26 (February 1971): 118.

568   "The Black Woman 1975." Black Scholar 6 (March 1975): see entire issue.

569 "Black Women in Politics." In National Roster of
     Black Elected Officials, Volume 6, edited by Joint
     Center for Political Studies. Washington, D.C.:
     Joint Center for Political Studies, 1976.

570 Blanchard, Paul D.   "Most School Board Members Are
     Their Own Men (and Women)--Not Conduits of the
     Public Will." American School Board Journal (May
     1974).

571 Blocker, J. S., Jr.   "Politics of Reform: Populists,
     Prohibition, and Woman Suffrage, 1891-1892."
     Historian 34 (August 1972): 614-632.

572 Boals, Kay.   "On Getting Feminine Qualities into the
     Power Structure." University: A Princeton
     Quarterly 54 (fall 1972): 6-12.

573 _____.   "The Politics of Male-Female Relations:
     The Functions of Feminist Scholarship." Signs:
     Journal of Women in Culture and Society 1 (fall
     1975): 161-174.

574 Board, John C.   "The Lady from Montana." Montana
     17 (1967): 2-17.

575 Booth, Alan.   "Sex and Social Participation." American
     Sociological Review 37 (April 1972): 183-192.

576 Borgersrode, M.   "She Wins on Her Record: Gladys
     Miller." Independent Woman 32 (November 1953):
     291.

577 Bourque, Susan C., and Grossholtz, Jean.   "Politics
     as Unnatural Practice: Political Science Looks at
     Female Participation." Politics and Society 4
     (winter 1974): 225-266.

578 Bowman, Lewis, and Boynton, G. R.   "Recruitment
     Patterns among Local Party Officials: A Model
     and Some Preliminary Findings in Selected Locales."
     American Political Science Review 60 (summer 1966):
     667-676.

579 Boyd, L. N.   "Salute to Our Congresswomen." Inde-
     pendent Woman 30 (October 1951): 70.

580   Boyd, Rosamonde Ramsey. "Women and Politics in
      the United States and Canada." Annals of the
      American Academy of Political and Social Science
      375 (January 1968): 52-57.

581   Brady, David W., and Tedin, Kent L. "Ladies in
      Pink: Religion and Political Ideology in the Anti-
      ERA Movement." Social Science Quarterly 56
      (March 1976): 564-575.

582   Brennan, Letitia. "How Women Can Break the Power
      Barrier." America (16 June 1973): 552-555.

583   "Brickerettes: Vigilant Women for the Bricker Amend-
      ment." Reporter 10 (2 March 1954): 2.

584   Britton, John H., Jr. "Black Women in Politics: Do
      We Have a Future?" Essence (March 1975): 80-89.

585   Broder, David S. "What Makes a Great Senator?"
      New York Times Magazine (14 June 1964).

586   Brooks, Gary H. "Women on City Councils: National
      Trends and Mississippi." Public Administration
      Survey 24 (September 1976): 1-5.

587   Brown, Connie, and Seitz, Jane. "You've Come a Long
      Way, Baby." In Sisterhood is Powerful: An An-
      thology of Writings from the Women's Liberation
      Movement, edited by Robin Morgan. New York:
      Random House, Vintage Books, 1970.

588   Brown, Nona B. "Inquiry Into the Feminine Mind."
      New York Times Magazine (12 April 1964).

589   _____. "Women's Vote: The Bigger Half?" New
      York Times Magazine (21 October 1956).

590   Brown, Robert H. "Composition of School Boards."
      American School Board Journal 129 (August 1954):
      23-24.

591   Brown, William H. "Sex Discrimination: It Isn't
      Funny, It is Illegal, and the Battle Has Just Begun."
      Good Government 88 (winter 1971): 18-21.

592   Brownmiller, Susan. "Sisterhood Is Powerful." New
      York Times Magazine (15 March 1970): 274.

593 Bryce, Herrington J., and Warrick, Allan. "Black Wo-
     men in Elective Office." Black Scholar 6 (October
     1974): 17-20.

594 _____, _____. "Black Women in Electoral
     Politics." Focus 9 (August 1973).

595 Buenker, J. D. "Urban Political Machine and Woman
     Suffrage: A Study in Political Adaptability." His-
     torian 33 (February 1971): 264-279.

596 Buhle, Mari Jo. "Socialist Women and the 'Girl
     Strikers,' Chicago, 1910." Signs: Journal of Wo-
     men in Culture and Society 1 (summer 1976): 1039-
     1052.

597 _____. "Women and the Socialist Party: 1901-1914."
     Radical America 4 (February 1972): 36-58.

598 Bullock, Charles S., and Heys, Patricia Findley.
     "Recruitment of Women for Congress: A Research
     Note." Western Political Science Quarterly 25
     (September 1972): 416-423.

599 Burnham, Sophy, and Knight, Janet. "The United States
     of America vs. Susan B. Anthony." Ms. 1 (Novem-
     ber 1972): 99.

600 Burris, Carol. "Politicking for Equality." Trial 9
     (November/December 1973): 23.

601 Burstein, Patricia, and Cimons, Marlene. "Women
     Candidates Who Won." Ms. 1 (March 1973): 68-71.

602 Calloway, DeVerne. "The Missouri Experience."
     FOCUS/Midwest 9 (1973): 20-21.

603 "Campaign '72: Women's Struggle for the Larger Role."
     Congressional Quarterly Weekly Report 30 (22 April
     1972): 883-885.

604 Carter, Luther J. "New Feminism: A Potent Force
     in Birth Control Policy." Science 167 (1970): 1234-
     1236.

605 Cartwright, M. "Lady Congressman from Ohio."
     Negro History Bulletin 17 (April 1954): 155-156.

606   Cates, John M., Jr.   "An Interview with Margaret
      Mead on the Woman Diplomat." Foreign Service
      Journal 46 (February 1969): 16.

607   Chandola, Harish. "New Position of Women." Eco-
      nomic and Political Weekly 8 (21 April 1973): 744-
      746.

608   Chase, Judy. "Inside HEW: Women Protest Sex Dis-
      crimination." Science 174 (15 October 1971): 270-
      274.

609   Cheshire, H. and Cheshire, M.   "Woman for Presi-
      dent?" New York Times Magazine (27 May 1956):
      60-61.

610   Cheshire, Maxine. "What Is Maggie Smith Up To?"
      Saturday Evening Post (18 April 1964): 30-32.

611   Chisholm, Shirley.   "The 51% Minority." Chicago:
      National Organization for Women (NOW).

612   _____. "Political Concerns of Women." National
      Association of Women Deans and Counselors Journal
      36 (fall 1972): 13-18.

613   _____. "The Politics of Coalition." Black Scholar
      4 (September 1972): 30-32.

614   _____. "Race, Revolution, and Women." Black
      Scholar 3 (December 1971): 17-21.

615   _____. "Sexism and Racism: One Battle to Fight."
      Personnel and Guidance Journal 51 (October 1972):
      123-125.

616   _____. "Why I Am Challenging in 1972." Signature
      (December 1971): 6.

617   _____. "Women Must Rebel." In Voices of the
      New Feminism, edited by Mary Lou Thompson.
      Boston: Beacon Press, 1970.

618   Chord, L. A. "Guardian of Our Gold." Independent
      Woman 32 (July 1953): 231-232.

619   Churchill, J. C., ed. "If Women Were in Control."
      Ladies Home Journal 67 (October 1950): 67.

620   "Cincinnati Women Ring Doorbells--Or How One Woman
      Got into Local Politics." National Municipal Re-
      view (now National Civic Review) 42 (March 1953):
      147-148.

621   "City Councilwomen: A Different Perspective."
      Nation's Cities 11 (September 1973): 24-31.

622   Clardy, M. L., and Alessi, F. V. "Helping the
      American Women to Step Outside Her Stereotypical
      Political Role." Social Science Record 3 (1975):
      3-6.

623   Coburn, Judith. "People: Dolores Huerta--La Pasio-
      naria of the Farmworkers." Ms. 5 (November 1976):
      11-18.

624   Coffin, Tris. "India Edwards: Queen-Maker of Wash-
      ington." Coronet 29 (April 1951): 124-128.

625   Cole, Margaret. "The Women's Vote: What Has It
      Achieved?" Political Quarterly 33 (January /Febru-
      ary /March 1962): 74-83.

626   Collier, Jane Fishburne. "Women in Politics." In
      Woman, Culture and Society, edited by Michelle
      Rosaldo and Louise Lamphere. Stanford, Calif.:
      Stanford University Press, 1974.

627   Collins, Huntly. "Betty Roberts of Oregon: Running
      and ... Running." Ms. 3 (October 1974): 83.

628   Colon, Frank T. "The Elected Woman." Social
      Studies 58 (November 1967): 256-261.

629   "Congress Has Record Number of Women." Congres-
      sional Quarterly Weekly Report 13 (23 December
      1955): 1310-1311.

630   "Congresswomen." Life 38 (17 January 1955): 36.

631   Connable, Rona. "Politics: A New Wide-Open World
      for Women." Mademoiselle 58 (March 1964): 164-
      167.

632   Connell, E. T. "Women Run the Rascals Out of Gary."
      American Magazine 149 (May 1950): 36-37.

633   Conway, Jill. "Jane Addams: An American Heroine."
      Daedalus (spring 1964).

634   Conway, M. Margaret, and Feigert, Frank B. "Motiva-
      tion, Incentive Systems, and the Political Party Or-
      ganization." American Political Science Review 72
      (December 1968): 1159-73.

635   Cook, Alice H. "Women and American Trade Unions."
      Annals of the Academy of Political and Social Science
      375 (January 1968): 125-132.

636   "Cool Headed Lady of the Crisis Bureau." Ebony 23
      (June 1968): 56-58.

637   Costantini, Edmond, and Craik, Kenneth H. "Women
      as Politicians: The Social Background, Personality,
      and Political Careers of Female Party Leaders."
      Journal of Social Issues 28 (1972): 217-236.

638   Costello, Mary. "Women Voters." Congressional
      Quarterly Editorial Research Reports (11 October
      1972): 767-784.

639   Cottin, Jonathan. "Comparing Slates in Illinois: Dif-
      fering Quotas for Women Delegates." National
      Journal (25 March 1972): 506-509.

640   Cottle, Thomas; Edwards, Carl; and Pleck, Joseph.
      "The Relationship of Sex Role Identity and Social
      and Political Attitudes." Journal of Personality 38
      (1970): 435-452.

641   Crawford, M. A. "Political Pioneering in California."
      Independent Woman 32 (February 1953): 44-46.

642   Cronin, Joseph. "Educating the Majority: A Woman-
      power Policy for the 1970's." Phi Delta Kappan 55
      (October 1973): 138-139.

643   Crosby, B. C. "Specialist in Municipal Government."
      Independent Woman 32 (February 1953): 41.

644   Crowley, Joyce. "Women Who Won the Right to Vote:
      The Suffragist Movement." Fourth International 16
      (spring 1955): 48-56.

645 Cummings, Judith. "Black Women in Public Office."
     Black Enterprise 5 (August 1974): 33-35.

646 Curran, C. "Woman Voter." Spectator 196 (6 January
     1956): 9-10.

647 Curtis, James. "Voluntary Association Joining: A
     Cross-National Comparative Note." American
     Sociological Review 36 (October 1971): 872-880.

648 Daley, R. J. et al. "The Woman Voter." Reviewing
     Stand (29 June 1952): 1-11.

649 "Data on Women in Public Office." Independent Woman
     34 (October 1955): 21.

650 Davenport, Walter. "Where Men Go Wrong About
     Women Voters." Colliers 138 (14 September 1956):
     82-84.

651 Davidson, Sara. "Foremothers." Esquire 80 (July
     1973): 71.

652 _____ . "The Girls on the Bandwagon." In Styles of
     Political Action in America, edited by Robert P.
     Wolff. New York: Random House, 1972.

653 _____ . "Girls on the Bandwagon: Political Girls
     on Capitol Hill." McCalls 97 (August 1970): 32-43.

654 _____ . "Militants for Women's Rights." Life (12
     December 1969).

655 _____ . "An 'Oppressed Majority' Demands Its
     Rights." Life (12 December 1969): 67.

656 Davis, Angela. "On Black Women." Ms. 1 (August
     1972): 55.

657 Davis, Susan. "Organizing from Within--Justice on the
     Job." Ms. 1 (August 1972): 92.

658 Dearden, John. "Sex-linked Differences in Political
     Behavior: An Investigation of their Possibly Innate
     Origins." Social Science Information 13 (April
     1974): 19-45.

659   DeCost, Dorothy K.   "Local Government's Role in Pro-
        gram to Advance the Status of Women." Municipal
        South 11 (April 1964): 20-21.

660   Degler, Carl N.   "The Changing Place of Women in
        America." Daedalus (spring 1964).

661   _____.   "Lost Women: Charlotte Perkins Gilman-
        The Economics of Victorian Morality." Ms. 1
        (June 1973): 22-28.

662   _____.   "Revolution Without Ideology: The Changing
        Place of Women in America." Daedalus 93 (spring
        1964): 653-670.

663   Dennis, Jack.   "Support for the Institution of Elections
        by the Mass Public." American Political Science
        Review 64 (September 1970): 819-835.

664   Devereaux, Edward C., Jr.   "Community Participation
        and Leadership." Journal of Social Issues 16:4
        (1960): 29-45.

665   _____.   "Neighborhood and Community Participation."
        Journal of Social Issues 16:4 (1960): 64-84.

666   "Did Women Elect Eisenhower?" U.S. News and World
        Report 34 (8 May 1953): 45-46.

667   Dinan, J., and Elliott, L.   "The Mayor Is No Angel."
        Reader s Digest 83 (July 1963): 154-157.

668   "Discussions: Women, Power and Politics." In Women
        and Men: Changing Roles, Relationships and Per-
        ceptions, edited by Libby A. Cater, Anne Firor
        Scott, and Wendy Martyna.   Palo Alto, Calif.: Aspen
        Institute for Humanistic Studies, 1976.

669   "Distaff Side: Eight Ladies of the 82nd Congress."
        Newsweek 37 (15 January 1951): 48.

670   Dixon, Marlene.   "Public Ideology and the Class Compo-
        sition of Women's Liberation (1966-1969)." Berkeley
        Journal of Sociology 16 (1971-72): 149-167.

671   Dobler, Lavinia.   "Esther Morris, Mother of Woman
        Suffrage." Westerner's Brandbook 4 (1956): 31.

672 Dodds, Harold W. "Women's Place in Politics."
Ladies Home Journal (August 1952).

673 Doing, Laura T. "Women on School Boards: Nine
Winners Tell How They Play the Game." American
School Board Journal 160 (March 1973): 34-40.

674 Donaldson, Alice. "Women Emerge as Political
Speakers." Speech Monographs 18 (March 1951):
54-61.

675 Dowse, Robert, and Hughes, John. "Girls, Boys, and
Politics." Berkeley Journal of Sociology 22 (March
1971): 53-67.

676 Dratch, Howard. "The Politics of Childcare in the
1940's." Science and Society 38 (summer 1974):
167-204.

677 Dreifus, C. "I Hope I'm Not a Token: New York's
Commissioner of Human Rights." McCalls 99
(October 1971): 51.

678 Dreifus, Claudia. "Interview with Patsy Mink."
M.B.A. (March 1972): 19.

679 _____. "Women in Politics: An Interview with
Edith Green." Social Policy (January/February
1972): 16-22.

680 Dubeck, Paula J. "Women and Access to Political
Office: A Comparison of Female and Male State
Legislators." Sociological Quarterly 17 (winter
1976): 42-52.

680a Dunlap, Mary C. "The Equal Rights Amendment in
the Courts." In Impact ERA: Limitations and Possibilities, edited by The California Commission on
the Status of Women. Millbrae, Calif.: Les
Femmes, 1976.

681 Dworkin, Susan. "Watch These Freshperson Congress-
persons." Ms. 3 (April 1975): 80-81.

682 Dyer, Louise. "The American School Board Member
and His- and Her-Era of Fierce New Independence."
American School Board Journal 160 (July 1973): 17-20.

683   East, Catherine. "What Do Women Want?" In What
       Is Happening to American Women, edited by Anne
       Firor Scott. Atlanta, Ga.: Southern Newspaper
       Publishers Association Foundation Seminar Books,
       1970.

684   Easton, David, and Dennis, Jack. "The Child's Acqui-
       sition of Regime Norms: Political Efficacy."
       American Political Science Review 61 (March 1967):
       25-38.

685   Eddy, Edward D. Jr. "What's the Use of Educating
       Women?" Saturday Review (18 May 1963).

686   Egan, J. "Up with Women in Politics." McCalls 98
       (September 1971): 47.

687   Ehrich, H. "State Department's Poetic Powerhouse:
       Kate Louchheim." Look 31 (17 October 1967): 118.

688   Eisenstein, Hester, and Sacks, Susan Riemer. "Wo-
       men in Search of Autonomy: An Action Design."
       Social Change 5 (1975): 4-6.

689   Eitzen, D. Stanley. "A Study of Voluntary Association
       Membership among Middle-Class Women." Rural
       Sociology 35 (March 1970): 84-91.

690   Eldersveld, Samuel. "The Independent Vote: Measure-
       ment, Characteristics, and Implications for Party
       Strategy." American Political Science Review 46
       (September 1952): 732-753.

691   Ellis, Katherine, and Petchesky, Rosalind. "Children
       of the Corporate Dream: An Analysis of Day Care
       as a Political Issue Under Capitalism." Socialist
       Revolution 2 (November/December 1972): 8-28.

692   Ellison, Jerome. "Is the U.S. Really Run by Women?"
       Saturday Evening Post (19 May 1951): 40-41.

693   "Enter, the Political Ladies." New York Times Maga-
       zine (19 October 1952): 12-13.

694   Ephron, Nora. "Women." Esquire 78 (November
       1972): 10.

695 "Equal Rights for Women? Things May Never Be the
Same." U.S. News and World Report 69 (24 August
1970): 29-30.

696 Erikson, Erik H. "Inner and Outer Space: Reflections
of Womanhood." Daedalus (spring 1964).

697 Erikson, Joan M. "Notes on the Life of Eleanor Roosevelt." Daedalus (spring 1964).

698 Eriksson-Joslyn, Kirsten. "A Nation of Volunteers:
Participatory Democracy or Administrative Manipula-
tion." Berkeley Journal of Sociology 18 (1973/1974):
159-181.

699 Erskine, Hazel. "The Polls: Women's Role." Public
Opinion Quarterly 35 (summer 1971): 275-290.

700 Estler, Suzanne E. "Women as Leaders in Public
Education." Signs: Journal of Women in Culture
and Society 1 (winter 1975): 363-356.

701 Etzioni, Amitai. "The Women's Movement--Tokens vs.
Objectives." Saturday Review (20 May 1972): 31-35.

702 "Eve's Operation: Women Delegates of the Democratic
Convention." Time 100 (24 July 1972): 25-26.

703 Eyde, Lorraine D. "The Status of Women in State and
Local Government." Public Personnel Management
2 (May/June 1973): 205-211.

704 Fairlie, Henry. "On the Humanity of Women." Public
Interest 23 (Spring 1971): 16-32.

705 Farah, Barbara G., and Hoag, Wendy. "The Changing
Status and Role of Women in Politics." In New
Research on Women at the University of Michigan:
Papers and Reports, edited by Dorothy Gies Mc-
Guigan. Ann Arbor, Mich.: University of Michigan,
Center for the Continuing Education of Women,
1974.

706 Farrell, Warren T. "Women's and Men's Liberation
Groups: Political Power Within the System and Out-
side the System." In Women in Politics, edited by
Jane S. Jaquette. New York: John Wiley, 1974.

707 Farris, Charles D. "Authoritarianism as a Political
     Behavior Variable." Journal of Politics 18 (February
     1956): 61-82.

708 Farson, Richard E. "The Rage of Women." Look 33
     (16 December 1969): 21-23.

709 Fasteau, Brenda Feigen, and Label, Bonnie. "Rating
     the Candidates: Feminists Vote the Rascals In or
     Out." Ms. (spring 1972): 74.

710 Ferdinand, Theodore N. "Psychological Femininity and
     Political Liberalism." Sociometry 27 (1964): 75-87.

711 Ferree, Myra Marx. "A Woman for President? Chang-
     ing Responses: 1958-1972." Public Opinion Quarterly
     38 (fall 1974): 390-399.

712 "Fight Against Women's Oppression Parallels Struggle
     Against Racism." Progressive Labor 9 (November
     1973): 24-29.

713 Figueroa, Ana. "Three Stages of the Convention on
     Political Rights of Women (as Passed in the United
     Nations Economic and Social Council Sessions)."
     United Nations Bulletin 13 (1 July 1952): 36-37.

714 Finifter, Ada W. "Dimensions of Political Alienation."
     American Political Science Review 64 (June 1970):
     389-425.

715 Finkelhor, Marion K. "Sex Discrimination and Local
     Government." Urban Lawyer 5 (spring 1973): 327-
     346.

716 "First Black Woman in the U.S. House of Representa-
     tives." Negro History Bulletin 33 (May 1970): 128.

717 "The First Ladies of South Dakota." South Dakota
     History 3 (1973): 156-168.

718 "First Woman Mayor in U.S. Reaches 100." American
     City 75 (May 1960): 23.

719 Fishel, Andrew, and Pottker, Janice. "School Boards
     and Sex Bias in American Education." Contemporary
     Education (winter 1974): 85-89.

720 Fisher, John. "Women Who Lay Down the Law."
     Chicago Sunday Tribune Magazine (12 January 1958):
     14.

721 "Five New Congresswomen." Family Planning/Popula-
     tion Reporter 2 (fall 1973): 14-16.

722 Fixx, James F. "Women, Politics, and the Future."
     Saturday Review 47 (20 June 1964): 22.

723 Flesch, N. "Her Honor, the Mayor, in 112 Cities."
     American City 80 (August 1965): 110.

724 "Flock of First Ladies and Maybe Ms. President."
     Life 71 (31 December 1971): 54-55.

725 Flora, Cornelia B., and Lynn, Naomi B. "Women and
     Political Socialization: Considerations of the Impact
     of Motherhood." In Women in Politics, edited by
     Jane S. Jaquette. New York: John Wiley, 1974.

726 Flynn, John P., and Webb, Gene E. "Women's Incen-
     tives for Community Participation in Policy Issues."
     Journal of Voluntary Action Research 4 (summer/
     fall 1975): 137-146.

727 Foley, Paul. "Whatever Happened to Women's Rights?"
     Atlantic Monthly 213 (March 1964): 63-65.

728 "Foot in Door." New Yorker 30 (6 March 1954): 19-20.

729 "Four Women Lead State Leagues of Municipalities."
     American City 70 (April 1955): 134.

730 Fowler, Marguerite Gilbert, and Van De Riet, Hani K.
     "Today and Yesterday: An Examination of the Femi-
     nist Personality." Journal of Psychology 82 (Novem-
     ber 1972): 269-276.

731 _____; Fowler, Robert L.; and Van De Riet, Hani
     K. "Feminism and Political Radicalism." Journal
     of Psychology 83 (March 1973): 237-242.

732 Frappollo, E. "At 91 Jeannette Rankin Is the Femi-
     nists' New Heroine." Life 72 (3 March 1972): 65.

733 Frappollo, Elizabeth. "The Ticket that Might Have

Been: Vice President Farenthold." Ms. 1 (January 1973): 74-76.

734   Freedman, Anne. "A Research Note on the Voluntary Association Participation of Political Activists." Journal of Voluntary Action Research 1 (1972): 54-56.

735   Freedman, Merven B. "Changes in Six Decades of Some Attitudes and Values Held by Educated Women." Journal of Social Issues 17 (1961): 19-28.

736   Freeman, Bonnie Cook. "Power, Patriarchy, and Political Primitives." In Women Scholars on Woman, edited by Joan I. Roberts. New York: David McKay, 1976.

737   Freeman, Jo. "The New Feminists." Nation 208 (24 February 1969): 241-244.

738   _____. "The Origins of the Women's Liberation Movement." American Journal of Sociology 78 (January 1973): 792-811.

739   _____. "The Political Impact of the Equal Rights Amendment." In Impact ERA: Limitations and Possibilities, edited by California Commission on the Status of Women. Millbrae, Calif.: Les Femmes, 1976.

740   _____. "The Politics of Women's Liberation: The Roots of Revolt." Intellect 103 (April 1975): 469-473.

741   _____. "Politics: Something DID Happen at the Democratic National Convention." Ms. 4 (October 1976): 74.

742   _____. "Review and Critique: The New Feminism." Nation (9 March 1974): 297-302.

743   _____. "Structure and Strategy in the Women's Liberation Movement." Urban and Social Change Review (May 1972): 71-74.

744   _____. "The Tyranny of Structurelessness." In Women in Politics, edited by Jane S. Jaquette. New York: John Wiley, 1974.

745 _____. "Women's Liberation and Its Impact on the
       Campus." Liberal Education 57 (December 1971):
       468-478.

746 _____. "The Women's Liberation Movement: Its
       Origins, Structures, Impact and Ideas." In Women:
       A Feminist Perspective, edited by Jo Freeman.
       Palo Alto, Calif.: Mayfield, 1975.

747 French, Eleanor C. "Key Political Force--The Ladies."
       New York Times Magazine (11 March 1956): 14.

748 Frenkel-Brunswick, Else. "Interaction of Psychological
       and Sociological Factors in Political Behavior."
       American Political Science Review 46 (March 1952):
       44-65.

749 "Fresh Blood for a Sick Congress." Life 73 (17 Novem-
       ber 1972): 42-48.

750 Friedan, Betty. "It's Nonsense That There Are No
       Qualified Women to Run for Office." McCalls 98
       (September 1971): 52.

751 _____. "Up from the Kitchen Floor." New York
       Times Magazine (4 March 1973): 8.

752 _____. "What Have Women Really Won?" McCalls
       (November 1972): 74.

753 Friggens, P. "What Wyoming Did for Women."
       Reader's Digest 77 (September 1960): 197-201.

754 Fry, A. "Along the Suffrage Trail." American West
       6 (January 1969): 16-25.

755 Fuller, B. "Why Women Will Rule the World." Mc-
       Calls 95 (March 1968): 10-11.

756 Galen, Marcy. "Lost Women: Harriet Tubman."
       Ms. 2 (August 1973): 16-18.

757 Gallagher, R. S. "Me for Ma, and I Ain't Got a Dern
       Thing Against Pa." American Heritage 17 (October
       1966): 46.

758 Gallas, Nesta M., ed. "A Symposium: Women in

Public Administration." Public Administration Review (July/August 1976): see entire issue.

759 Gardiner, Lady. "Some More Equal Than Others."
     Contemporary Review 220 (January 1972): 32-36.

760 Gehlen, Frieda L. "Women in Congress: Their Power
     and Influence in a Man's World." Transaction 6
     (October 1969): 36-40.

761 Geis, Florence L. "Why Not a Woman for President?
     The Psychology of Sex Role Expectation." In The
     Role of Women in Politics, edited by Mae R. Carter.
     Newark, Del.: University of Delaware, Division of
     Continuing Education, 1964.

762 "Gentlewoman from Maine: Margaret Chase Smith."
     Ladies Home Journal 78 (January 1961): 65.

763 "Gentlewomen." Life 37 (15 January 1951): 48.

764 Gittelson, N. "Which Ms. Has the Movement? Betty
     and Gloria and Shirley and Bella." Harper's Bazaar
     105 (July 1972): 80-81.

765 Glenn, Norval D., and Grimes, Michael. "Aging,
     Voting, and Political Interest." American Sociologi-
     cal Review 33 (August 1968): 563-575.

766 Gold, Doris. "Women and Voluntarism." In Woman in
     Sexist Society: Studies in Power and Powerlessness,
     edited by Vivian Gornick and Barbara Moran. New
     York: Basic Books, 1971.

767 Goldstein, Mark L. "Blue-Collar Women and American
     Labor Unions." Industrial and Labor Relations Forum
     7 (October 1971): 1-35.

768 Goodman, Ellen. "People: Louise Day Hicks--"When
     They Call Me a Racist, I Don't Listen...." Ms. 4
     (January 1976): 99-103.

769 "Goodwill Toward Women." New Republic 165 (25 De-
     cember 1971): 5-6.

770 Gordon, Ann D.; Buhle, Mari Jo; and Schrom, Nancy
     E. "Women in American Society: An Historical

Contribution." Radical America 4 (July/August 1971): 3-66.

771 Gordon, Linda. "Are the Interests of Men and Women Identical?" Signs: Journal of Women in Culture and Society 1 (summer 1976): 1011-1018.

772 Gould, B. B. "Appointment for Women." Ladies Home Journal 78 (January 1961): 64.

773 Gouldner, Helen P. "Dimensions of Organizational Commitment." Administrative Science Quarterly 4 (May 1960): 468-490.

774 Gove, Walter, and Costner, Herbert. "Organizing the Poor: An Evaluation of a Strategy." Social Science Quarterly 50 (December 1969): 643-656.

775 Grafton, Samuel. "Women in Politics: The Coming Breakthrough." McCalls (September 1962): 102-103.

776 Graham, Lee. "Who's in Charge Here? Not Women!" New York Times Magazine (2 September 1962): 8.

777 Grant, Joanne. "Mississippi Politics--A Day in the Life of Ella T. Baker." In The Black Woman: An Anthology, edited by Toni Cade. New York: Signet, 1970.

778 Green, Arnold W., and Melnick, Eleanor. "What Has Happened to the Feminist Movement." In Studies in Leadership: Leadership and Democratic Action, edited by Alvin W. Gouldner. New York: Harper, 1950.

779 Greenfield, Jeff. "Women in Politics." 4 part syndicated newspaper story. (Collection of the Center for the American Woman and Politics.)

780 Greenstein, Fred I. "Sex-Related Political Differences in Childhood." Journal of Politics 23 (May 1961): 353-371.

781 Greer, Germaine. "McGovern, The Big Tease." Harpers (October 1972): 56-71.

782 Griffiths, Martha. "The Law Must Reflect the New

Image of Women." Hastings Law Journal 23 (November 1971): 1-14.

783 _____ . "Women and Legislation." In Voices of the New Feminism, edited by Mary Lou Thompson. Boston: Beacon Press, 1970.

784 Gruberg, Martin. "The Impact of Women on 1972 American Politics." Women Speaking 3 (January 1973): 8-9.

785 _____ . "Spotlight on Women." Oshkosh (Wisc.) Northwestern 1971-1973. (A series of newspaper articles on women and politics.)

786 Gunderson, R. G. "Tippecanoe Belles of 1840." American Heritage 1 (September 1952): 3-5.

787 Gusfield, Joseph R. "Social Structures and Moral Reform: A Study of the Women's Christian Temperance Union." American Journal of Sociology 61 (November 1955): 221-232.

788 Hacker, Helen. "Women as a Minority Group." Social Forces (1951): 7.

789 Hammond, Nancy, and Belote, Glenda. "From Deviance to Legitimacy: Women as Political Candidates." University of Michigan Papers in Women's Studies 1 (June 1974): 58-72.

790 Hanawalt, Ella. "What Is the Role of Women in Community Leadership?" Reviewing Stand (17 August 1952): 1-11.

791 Hansen, Susan B.; Franz, Linda M.; and Netemeyer-Mays, Margaret. "Women's Political Participation and Policy Preferences." Social Science Quarterly 56 (March 1976): 576-590.

792 Harris, Louis. "Newsweek Poll: The Women's Vote." Newsweek 64 (21 September 1964): 32.

793 Harris, Ted Carlton. "Jeannette Rankin in Georgia." Georgia Historical Quarterly 58 (spring 1974): 55-78.

794 Harry, Joseph. "Family Localism and Social

Participation." American Journal of Sociology 75
(March 1970): 821-827.

795 Hartley, Ruth. "Children's Concept of Male and Female
Roles." Merrill-Palmer Quarterly 6 (1960): 153-163.

796 Hastings, Philip K. "Hows and Howevers of the Women
Voter." New York Times Magazine (12 June 1960):
14.

797 "Hawaii's Top Woman Politician." Ebony 18 (April
1963): 51-52.

798 Heilbrun, Carolyn. "Eleanor: The Years Alone."
Ms. 1 (October 1972): 30-32.

799 Heiskanen, Veronica Stolte. "Sex Roles, Social Class
and Political Consciousness." Acta Sociologica 14
(1971): 83-95.

800 _____, and Haavio-Mannila, Elina. "The Position
of Women in Society: Formal Ideology vs. Everyday
Ethic." Social Science Information 6 (1967): 169-188.

801 Helms, Winifred. "Equal Rights, Where Do We Stand?"
AAUW Journal 46 (March 1953): 165.

802 "Help Wanted." Newsweek 80 (21 August 1972): 16-17.

803 Henderson, Julie. "Impact of the World Social Situation on Women." Annals of the Academy of Political
and Social Science 375 (January 1968): 44-51.

804 Hendry, A. B. "Angry Wives of Gary." Coronet 30
(June 1951): 40-43.

805 Henley, Nancy. "Power, Sex, and Non-Verbal Communication." Berkeley Journal of Sociology 17 (1973):
1-26.

806 "Here's How: Qualified Women in Policy Making Posts."
Independent Woman 30 (March 1951): 86.

807 "Her Honor Takes the Bench." Time 85 (29 January
1965): 41.

808 "Her Honor the Mayor." Good Housekeeping 145
(November 1957): 14.

809   Hickey, M.   "Politics Without Malice: Panel Discus-
        sion."   Ladies Home Journal 81 (April 1964): 80.

810   _____.   "To Make Your Vote Count."   Ladies Home
        Journal 69 (January 1952): 48.

811   "Highlights of Luncheon for Women in Government."
        National Business Woman 38 (February 1959):13-17.

812   Hinckle, Warren, and Hinckle, Marrianne.   "A History
        of the Rise of the Unusual Movement for Women
        Power in the United States, 1961-1968."   Ramparts
        (February 1968): 24.

813   Hirsch, Eleanor.   "Grandma Felton and the U.S.
        Senate."   Mankind 4 (1974): 53-57.

814   Hochschild, Arlie.   "The Role of the Ambassador's
        Wife: An Exploratory Study."   Journal of Marriage
        and the Family 31 (February 1969): 73-87.

815   _____, ed.   "The American Woman."   Transaction 8
        (November/December 1970): see entire issue.

816   Hodge, R. W., and Treiman, D. J.   "Social Participa-
        tion and Social Status."   American Sociological Re-
        view 33 (October 1968): 722-740.

817   Hoffman, Lois Wladis.   "Early Childhood Experiences
        and Women's Achievement Motives."   Journal of
        Social Issues 28 (1972): 129-156.

818   Holden, Constance.   "Women in Michigan: Parlaying
        Rights into Power."   Science 178 (1 December 1972):
        962-965.

819   Holly, H.   "Some Women Who Won Tell How to Run."
        Woman's Home Companion 82 (July 1955): 18.

820   Holter, Harriet.   "Sex Roles and Social Change."   In
        Toward a Sociology of Women, edited by Constantina
        Safilios-Rothschild.   Lexington, Mass.: Xerox Col-
        lege, 1972.

821   Holtzman, Abraham.   "Campaign Politics: A New Role
        for Women."   Southwestern Social Science Quarterly
        (now Social Science Quarterly) 40 (March 1960): 314-
        320.

822   Hope, S. C. "Practical Politics for the Working Wo-
      man." National Business Woman 39 (February 1960):
      4-5.

823   Hottel, Althea K., ed. "Women Around the World."
      Annals of the American Academy of Political and
      Social Science 375 (January 1968): see entire issue.

824   Howard, J. "Shaker-Upper Wants to be Madame Presi-
      dent Chisholm." Life 71 (5 November 1971): 81.

825   "However, Maine Goes--It Goes Feminine." New York
      Times Magazine (23 October 1960): 20.

826   "How to De-radicalize; Republican National Convention."
      Time 100 (4 September 1972): 17-18.

827   "How Women Are Doing in Politics." U.S. News and
      World Report 69 (7 September 1970): 24-27.

828   Hubbell, Thelma Lee, and Lothrop, Gloria R. "The
      Friday Morning Club, a Los Angeles Legacy."
      Southern California Quarterly 50 (1968): 59-90.

829   Huber, Joan, ed. "Changing Women in a Changing
      Society: A Special Issue." American Journal of
      Sociology 78 (January 1973): see entire issue.

830   "If I Were President; Sixteen Famous Women Give
      Their Program for America." McCalls 95 (January
      1968): 51-53.

831   Iglitzin, Lynne B. "A Case Study in Patriarchal Poli-
      tics: Women on Welfare." American Behavioral
      Science 17 (March 1974): 487-506.

832   _____. "The Making of Apolitical Woman: Feminity
      and Sex-Stereotyping in Girls." In Women in Poli-
      tics, edited by Jane S. Jaquette. New York: John
      Wiley, 1974.

833   _____. "Political Education and Sexual Liberation."
      Politics and Society 2 (winter 1972): 241-254.

834   Israel, Lee. "Helen Gahagan Douglas." Ms. 2 (Octo-
      ber 1973): 55-59.

835   "It's 'No Accident' that Men Outnumber Women on

School Boards Nine to One." American School Board Journal (May 1974): 53.

836   Jaquette, Jane S.   "Review Essay: Political Science."
      Signs: Journal of Women in Culture and Society 2
      (autumn 1976): 147-164.

837   Jennings, M. Kent, and Langton, Kenneth P.   "Mothers
      vs. Fathers: The Formation of Political Orienta-
      tions Among Young Americans."   Journal of Politics
      31 (May 1968): 329.

838   _____, and Niemi, Richard G.   "The Division of
      Political Labor Between Mothers and Fathers."
      American Political Science Review 65 (March 1971):
      69-82.

839   _____, and Thomas, Norman.   "Men and Women in
      Party Elites: Social Roles and Political Resources."
      Midwest Journal of Political Science 7 (November
      1968): 469-492.

840   Jensen, J. M.   "Annette Abbott Adams, Politician."
      Pacific Historical Review 35 (May 1966): 185-201.

841   Johnson, Dorothy E.   "Organized Women as Lobbyists
      in the 1920's."   Capitol Studies 1 (spring 1972): 41-58.

842   Johnson, G. W.   "Dynamic Victoria Woodhull."   Ameri-
      can Heritage 7 (June 1956): 44-47.

843   Johnson, K. R.   "Kate Gordon and the Woman-Suffrage
      Movement in the South."   Journal of Southern History
      38 (August 1972): 365-392.

844   Jones, Dorcey D.   "Catherine Campbell Cunningham,
      Advocate for Equal Rights for Women."   Arkansas
      Historical Quarterly 12 (summer 1953): 85-90.

845   Joreen.   "The 51% Minority Group: A Statistical Essay."
      In Sisterhood Is Powerful: An Anthology of Writings
      from the Women's Liberation Movement, edited by
      Robin Morgan.   New York: Random House, Vintage
      Books, 1970.

846   Joslyn, Kerstin.   "A Nation of Volunteers: Participa-
      tory Democracy or Administrative Manipulation?"
      Berkeley Journal of Sociology 18 (1973-1974): 159-181.

847 _____, and Sommers, Tish. "Volunteerism and the
       Status of Women: A Position Paper." In Volunteer
       Beware: Guidelines for Discussion, edited by the
       Task Force on Women and Volunteerism. Chicago:
       National Organization for Women, 1971.

848 Julianelli, Jane. "Lost Women: Bessie Hillman--Up
       from the Sweatshop." Ms. 1 (May 1973): 16-20.

849 Kahn, E. J., Jr. "Thank You, Madam President;
       Dancing at the White House." New Yorker 40 (2
       May 1964): 103-104.

850 Karnig, Albert K., and Walter, B. Oliver. "Elections
       of Women to City Councils." Social Science Quar-
       terly 56 (March 1976): 605-613.

851 Kayden, Xandra. "A Speculation--Politics and Sexu-
       ality." Harvard Political Review 4 (spring 1976):
       11-16.

852 Keller, Suzanne. "The Future Status of Women in
       America." Demographic and Social Aspects of Popu-
       lation Growth 1: 269-287. (Commission on Population
       Growth and the American Future, Research Reports.)

853 Kenworthy, J. "Treasurer of the Giant of Cities."
       National Business Woman 39 (September 1960): 6-7.

854 Kern, Edward. "The 'Woman Problem.' Part II."
       Life (21 August 1971): 41.

855 _____. "Women's Fight for the Vote." Life 71 (20
       August 1971): 40-50.

856 Kerr, B. W. "Opening a Window in the Smoke-Filled
       Room: New York County Democratic Women's Work-
       shop." Reporter 14 (12 January 1956): 22-25.

857 Kerr, Virginia. "Vote Early, Vote Often: The ABCs
       of Delegate Selection." Ms. 4 (January 1976): 95-98.

858 _____, and Sudow, Ellen. "Call to Action: A Legis-
       lative Agenda for the 93rd Congress." Ms. 1 (Janu-
       ary 1973): 81-85.

859 Kessler-Harris, Alice. "The Autobiography of Ann

Washington Craton." Signs: Journal of Women in
Culture and Society 1 (summer 1976): 1019-1038.

860   Keyek, Eugene. "A Second Look at School Board
      Members." New Jersey School Leader (May/June
      1974): 27.

861   _____. "A Second Look at School Board Members."
      New Jersey School Leader (July/August 1974): 44.

862   _____. "A Second Look at School Board Members."
      New Jersey School Leader (September/October
      1974): 24.

863   King, Mae C. "Oppression and Power: The Unique
      Status of the Black Woman in the American Political
      System." Social Science Quarterly 56 (June 1975):
      116-128.

864   _____. "The Politics of Sexual Stereotypes." Black
      Scholar (March/April 1973): 12-23.

865   Kinkead, Katharine T. "We Darn Near Killed Luella."
      New Yorker (5 May 1956): 118.

866   Kirkpatrick, Jeane. "Representation in the American
      National Conventions: The Case of 1972." British
      Journal of Political Science 5 (July 1975): 265-322.

867   "Kiss of the Muse, Kate Louchheim's State Appointment."
      Newsweek 68 (17 October 1966): 32.

868   Kitt, Alice S. and David B. Gleicher. "Determinants
      of Voting Behavior." Public Opinion Quarterly 14
      (fall 1950): 393-412.

869   Klotzburger, Kay. "Political Action By Academic
      Women." In Academic Women on the Move, edited
      by Alice S. Rossi and Ann Calderwood. New York:
      Russell Sage Foundation, 1973.

870   Knapp, Betty, and Guyol, Mary Ann. "Learning By
      Doing with the LWV." Journal of Social Issues
      16:1 (1960): 57-65.

871   Knudsen, Dean D. "The Declining Status of Women:
      Popular Myths and the Failure of Functionalist
      Thought." Social Forces 48 (1969): 183-193.

872   Kohlmeier, Louis M. "Justice Report/Detroit's
        Cornelia Kennedy is Top Supreme Court Possibility."
        National Journal Reports 7 (10 May 1975): 690-691.

873   Kolmer, E. "Nineteenth Century Woman's Rights Move-
        ment: Black and White." Negro History Bulletin
        35 (December 1970): 178-180.

874   Kontopoulos, Kyriakos M. "Women's Liberation as a
        Social Movement." In Toward a Sociology of Women,
        edited by Constantina Safilios-Rothschild. Lexington,
        Mass.: Xerox College, 1972.

875   Kramer, Jane. "Profiles: Founding Cadre; Personali-
        ties of and Dialogues Among Some Members of a
        Woman's Liberation Group." New Yorker 46 (28
        November 1970): 52.

876   Kramer, Philip. "The Indigenous Worker: Hometowner,
        Striver, or Activist." Social Work 17 (January 1972):
        43-49.

877   Krauss, Wilma Rule. "The Political Implications of
        Gender Roles: A Review of the Literature." Ameri-
        can Political Science Review 68 (December 1974):
        1706-1723.

878   Kruscke, Earl R. "Level of Optimism as Related to
        Female Political Behavior." Social Science 41
        (April 1966): 67-75.

879   Kuhn, Irene Corbally. "Our Five Enduring Women:
        Smith, Kennedy, Buckley, Luce, Mesta." Family
        Weekly (1 August 1971): 5-6.

880   _____ . "Women Don't Belong in Politics." Ameri-
        can Mercury (August 1953): 3-6.

881   LaCossitt, Henry. "The Mayor Wears Flowers in Her
        Hair." Saturday Evening Post 226 (22 May 1954):
        38-39.

882   LaCoste, R. "Petticoat Government Suits This Town."
        Independent Woman 32 (June 1953): 193.

883   "Ladies' Day; New Appointments." Time 83 (13 March
        1964): 22-23.

884 "Ladies in the Club." New Republic 143 (10 October
     1960): 6.

885 "Ladies Lunch: Forty-Seventh Annual Luncheon of the
     Women's National Republican Club." New Yorker
     43 (10 February 1968): 25-26.

886 "Lady from Maine." Newsweek 35 (12 June 1950): 24-
     26.

887 Lambright, W. Henry. "Womanpower: The Next Step
     in Manpower Policy." Public Personnel Review
     (January 1970): 27-30.

888 Langer, Elinor. "Why Big Business is Trying to Defeat
     the ERA - The Economic Implications of Equality."
     Ms. 4 (May 1976): 64.

889 Lansing, Marjorie. "The American Woman: Voter and
     Activist." In Women in Politics, edited by Jane S.
     Jaquette. New York: John Wiley, 1974.

890 _____. "Political Change for the American Woman."
     In Women in the World: A Comparative Study, edited
     by Lynne B. Iglitzen and Ruth Ross. Santa Barbara,
     Calif.: Clio Books, 1976.

891 _____. "Women: The New Political Class." In
     A Sampler of Women's Studies, edited by Doro-
     thy McGuigan. Ann Arbor: University of Michi-
     gan, Center for Continuing Education of Women,
     1973.

892 Larson, T. A. "Dolls, Vassals, and Drudges--Pioneer
     Women in the West." Western Historical Quarterly
     3 (January 1972): 5-16.

893 LaRue, Linda J. M. "Black Liberation and Women's
     Lib." Transaction 8 (November/December 1970):
     59-64.

894 Lash, Joseph. "The Roosevelts and Arthurdale."
     Washington Monthly 3 (November 1971): 22-38.

895 Lawrence, D. "Should a Woman be on the Supreme
     Court?" U.S. News and World Report 71 (25
     October 1971): 104.

896 _____. "Why and Why Not a Woman for President?" U.S. News and World Report 56 (17 February 1964): 108.

897 "The Law: Up from Coverture." Time 99 (20 March 1972): 67-68.

898 Lawrenson, Helen. "The Feminine Mistake." Esquire (January 1971): 83.

899 Leader, Shelah Gilbert. "Women Candidates for Elective Office: A Case Study." In The Role of Women in Politics, edited by Mae R. Carter. Newark, Del.: University of Delaware, Division of Continuing Education, 1964.

900 "League of Women Voters." Ebony 21 (October 1966): 107-108.

901 Lear, Martha Weinman. "Five Passionate Feminists." McCalls (July 1970): 52.

902 _____. "The Second Feminist Wave: What Do These Women Want?" New York Times Magazine (10 March 1968): 24.

903 Lee, Percy Maxim. "Why Not More Women in Public Office?" National Municipal Review (now National Civic Review) 43 (June 1954): 307-308.

904 Lepper, Mary. "A Study of Career Structures of Federal Executives: A Focus on Women." In Women in Politics, edited by Jane S. Jaquette. New York: Wiley, 1974.

905 Lerner, Gerda. "Sarah M. Grimke's 'Sisters of Charity'." Signs: Journal of Women in Culture and Society 1 (autumn 1975): 246-256.

906 _____. "Women's Rights and American Feminism." American Scholar (spring 1971): 235-248.

907 Leven, Helene. "Organizational Affiliation and Powerlessness: A Case Study of the Welfare Poor." Social Problems 16 (summer 1968): 18-32.

908 Levine, Daniel. "Jane Addams: Romantic Radical, 1889-1912." Mid-America 44 (1962): 195-210.

909   Levitt, Morris Jacob. "The Political Role of American
      Women." Journal of Human Relations 15 (first
      quarter 1967): 23-35.

910   Lewis, F. "New Frontier Women." Saturday Evening
      Post 235 (17 March 1962): 36.

911   Lewis, Linda, and Baedeme, Sally. "The Women's
      Liberation Movement." In New Left Thought: An
      Introduction, edited by Lyman T. Sargent. Home-
      wood, Ill.: Dorsey Press, 1972.

912   Lipman-Blumen, Jean. "How Ideology Shapes Women's
      Lives." Scientific American 226 (1972): 34-42.

913   _____. "Role De-Differentiation as a System Re-
      sponse to Crisis: Occupational and Political Roles
      of Women." Sociological Inquiry 43 (1973): 105-129.

914   Lipset, Seymour M., et al. "The Psychology of
      Voting: An Analysis of Political Behavior." In
      Handbook of Social Psychology, vol. 2, 2d ed., edited
      by Gardner Lindzey and Elliot Aronson. Reading,
      Mass.: Addison-Wesley, 1968.

915   Lisagor, P., and Higgins, M. "L.B.J.'s Hunt for
      Womanpower." Saturday Evening Post 237 (27 June
      1964): 86-87.

916   Lockett, E. B. "She-Town." Colliers 126 (4 November
      1950): 20-21.

917   Louchheim, Kate. "Women in the Service of Community
      and Nation." Department of State Bulletin 50 (2
      March 1964): 347-349.

918   Louis, James P. "Sue Shelton White and the Woman
      Suffrage Movement in Tennessee, 1913-1920."
      Tennessee Historical Quarterly 22 (1963): 170-190.

919   Luce, Claire Boothe. "Without Portfolio; Committee
      Chairmanships." McCalls 87 (February 1960): 16.

920   Lyford, K. V. E. "Diplomacy by Jeep." Independent
      Woman 31 (December 1952): 358-360.

921   Lynd, S. "Jane Addams and the Radical Impulse."
      Commentary 32 (July 1951): 54-59.

922   Lynden, Patricia. "The Plot Thickens: What Happens
      When There Are Two Good Women and Two Good
      Men--All in the Same Race?" Ms. 3 (October 1974):
      76.

923   Lynn, Naomi B. "Women in Politics: An Overview."
      In Women: A Feminist Perspective, edited by Jo
      Freeman. Palo Alto, Calif.: Mayfield, 1975.

924   _____, and Flora, Cornelia B. "Motherhood and
      Political Participation: The Changing Sense of Self."
      Journal of Political and Military Sociology 1 (spring
      1973): 91-103.

925   Maccoby, Eleanor; Matthews, Richard E.; and Morton,
      Anton S. "Youth and Political Change." Public
      Opinion Quarterly 18 (spring 1954): 23-39.

926   Maccoby, Herbert. "The Differential Political Activity
      of Participants in a Volunteer Association." Ameri-
      can Sociological Review 23 (October 1958): 524-532.

927   McCormack, Thelma. "Toward a Nonsexist Perspective
      on Social and Political Change." In Another Voice:
      Perspectives on Social Life and Social Science, edited
      by Marcia Millman and Rosabeth Moss Kanter. New
      York: Doubleday, Anchor Press, 1975.

928   McDonald, Donald. "The Liberation of Women." Center
      Magazine 5 (May/June 1972): 25-44.

929   McDowell, Margaret B. "The New Rhetoric of Woman
      Power." Midwest Quarterly 12 (winter 1971): 187-
      198.

930   McFadden, Judith Nies. "Women's Lib on Capitol Hill."
      Progressive 34 (December 1970): 22-25.

931   McFarland, C. K. "Crusade for Child Laborers:
      'Mother' Jones and the March of the Mill Children."
      Pennsylvania History 38 (July 1971): 283-296.

932   McGrath, Wilma E., and Soule, John W. "Rocking the
      Cradle or Rocking the Boat: Women at the 1972
      Democratic National Convention." Social Science
      Quarterly 55 (June 1974): 141-150.

933   MacInnis, Grace.   "Women and Politics."   Parliamen-
      tarian 53 (January 1972): 8-12.

934   McKee, John P., and Sherriffs, Alex C.   "Men's and
      Women's Beliefs, Ideals and Self-Concepts."   Ameri-
      can Journal of Sociology 64 (January 1959): 356-363.

935   MacLaine, Shirley.   "Women, the Convention and Brown
      Paper Bags."   New York Times Magazine (30 July
      1972): 14.

936   MacPherson, Hugh.   "The Politics of Sexual Discrimina-
      tion."   Spectator 228 (1 January 1972): 6.

937   McQuatters, G. F.   "Women in the 82nd Congress."
      Independent Woman 30 (January 1951): 2-4.

938   McWilliams, Nancy.   "Contemporary Feminism, Con-
      sciousness-Raising and Changing Views of the Politi-
      cal."   In Women in Politics, edited by Jane S.
      Jaquette.   New York: John Wiley, 1974.

939   "Madam President."   Time 99 (20 March 1972): 34.

940   Malone, James E.   "Minorities, Women, and Young
      People in Local Government."   Public Management
      55 (May 1973): 5.

941   Mandel, Ruth.   "Political Woman: Public Role and
      Personal Challenges."   Carnegie Quarterly 22 (sum-
      mer 1974): 1-5.

942   March, James G.   "Husband-Wife Interaction Over
      Political Issues."   Public Opinion Quarterly 17
      (winter 1953): 461-470.

943   Marcus, Barbara.   "The Year of the Women Candidates."
      Ms. 1 (September 1972): 64-69.

944   Markel, Helen.   "Twenty-Four Hours in the Life of
      Margaret Chase Smith."   McCalls (May 1964).

945   Marr, J.   "Women in State Departments of Education."
      Phi Delta Kappan 55 (October 1973): 142-143.

946   Marshall, Dale Rogers, and Anderson, Janell.   "Imple-
      mentations and the Equal Rights Amendment."   In

Impact ERA: Limitations and Possibilities, edited
by California Commission on the Status of Women.
Millbrae, Calif.: Les Femmes, 1976.

947 Mason, Karen Oppenheim, and Bumpass, Larry L.
"U.S. Women's Sex-Role Ideology, 1970." American
Journal of Sociology 80 (1975): 1212-1219.

948 _____; Czajka, John L.; and Arber, Sara.
"Change in U.S. Women's Sex-Role Attitudes."
American Sociological Review 41 (August 1976):
573-596.

949 Mayer, J. "Let's Put Women in Their Place Like, for
Instance, City Hall." McCalls 98 (February 1971):
74.

950 Mead, Margaret. "Must Women Be Bored with Politics?" Redbook 123 (October 1964): 20.

951 _____. "Women and Politics." Redbook 136 (November 1970): 50.

952 Mednick, Martha Shuch, and Tangri, Sandra Schwartz.
"New Perspectives on Women." Journal of Social
Issues 28:2 (1972): see entire issue.

953 Meiklejohn, D. "Jane Addams and American Democracy." Social Science Review 34 (September 1960):
253-264.

954 Menon, Lakshmi N. "From Constitutional Recognition
to Public Office." Annals of the American Academy
of Political and Social Science 375 (January 1968):
34-43.

955 Mikulski, Barbara. "How We Lost the Election
But Won the Campaign." Ms. 4 (July 1975):
59.

956/7 Miller, Jean Baker. "On Women: New Political
Directions for Women." Social Policy 2 (July/
August 1971): 32.

958 Miller, Judy Ann. "The Representative Is a Lady."
Black Politician 1 (fall 1969): 17-18.

959   Miller, Mungo.   "The Waukegan Study of Voter Turnout
        Prediction."   Public Opinion Quarterly 16 (fall 1952):
        381-398.

960   Millett, Kate.   "On Angela Davis."   Ms. 1 (August
        1972): 54.

961   _____.   "On Angela Davis."   (Part II) Ms. 1 (Sep-
        tember 1972): 58.

962   Minnis, Mhyra S.   "Cleavage in Women's Organizations:
        A Reflection of the Social Structure of a City."
        American Sociological Review 18 (February 1953):
        47-53.

963   _____.   "The Patterns of Women's Organizations:
        Significance, Types, Social Prestige, Rank and Ac-
        tivities."   In Community Structure and Analysis,
        edited by Marvin B. Sussman.   New York: Thomas
        Crowell, 1959.

964   Miscossi, Anita L.   "Conversion to Women's Lib."
        Transaction 8 (November/December 1970): 82-90.

965   Mohr, Judith.   "Why Not More Women City Managers?"
        Public Management 55 (1973): 13-15.

966   Moore, Emily C.   "Abortion and Public Policy: What
        Are the Issues?"   New York Law Forum 17 (1971):
        411-436.

967   Moore, Joan W.   "Exclusiveness and Ethnocentrism in
        a Metropolitan Upper-Class Agency."   Pacific Socio-
        logical Review 5 (spring 1962): 16-20.

968   _____.   "Patterns of Women's Participation in Volun-
        tary Associations."   American Journal of Sociology
        66 (May 1961): 592-598.

969   "More BPWs in Policy Making Posts."   Independent
        Woman 33 (June 1954): 202-203.

970   "More Than Orchid-Bearers."   Time 60 (24 November
        1952): 20-21.

971   More, W.   "Nun for Congress."   America 115 (17
        December 1966): 797.

972 "More Women in Top Government Jobs." U.S. News
     and World Report 56 (16 March 1964): 19.

973 Morgan, Jan. "Women and Political Socialization:
     Fact and Fantasy in Easton and Dennis and in Lane."
     Politics 9 (May 1974): 50-55.

974 Morris, Ann. "Women Fare Well on Appointment to
     the Judiciary but Promotions Are Rare." California
     Journal (May 1973): 160-161.

975 Morris, Monica B. "The Public Definition of a Social
     Movement: Women's Liberation." Sociology and
     Social Research 54 (1973): 526-543.

976 Morrison, A. "Top Woman Civil Rights Lawyer."
     Ebony 18 (January 1963): 50-52.

977 Morrissey, Michael W. "Sex(ism) and the School Board
     Member." Phi Delta Kappan 50 (October 1973): 142.

978 Motley, Constance Baker. "Constitution: Key to Free-
     dom." Ebony 18 (September 1963): 221-222.

979 Mueller, Marnie W. "Economic Determinants of
     Volunteer Work by Women." Signs: Journal of
     Women in Culture and Society 1 (winter 1975): 325-
     338.

980 Mullins, Carolyn. "If Superintendents Could Pick Their
     Own School Board Members, Here's the Kind They
     Say They'd Choose." American School Board Journal
     161 (September 1974): 25-29.

981 _____. "The Plight of the Boardwoman: The Fe-
     male School Board Member Still Has a Tough Time
     of It." American School Board Journal 159 (Febru-
     ary 1972): 27-32.

982 "Negro Women in Politics." Ebony 21 (August 1966):
     96-100.

983 Nelson, A. D. "First Ladies of the Ballot Box."
     American Mercury 90 (March 1960): 57-58.

984 Neuberger, Maurine. "Footnotes on Politics by a Lady
     Legislator." New York Times Magazine (27 May
     1951): 18.

985 Neuberger, Richard L. "My Wife Succeeds at Politics,
     Too." Coronet 33 (November 1952): 36-38.

986 "Never Underestimate." Newsweek (26 July 1971):
     29-30.

987 "Newcomers in the House." Time 96 (16 November
     1970): 27.

988 "Newer Voices Are Being Heard...." AAUW Journal
     69 (November 1975): 22.

989 "New Head for Women's Bureau Takes Place." Inde-
     pendent Woman 33 (January 1954): 3-4.

990 Nies, Judith. "The Abzug Race: A Lesson in Politics."
     Ms. 1 (February 1973): 76.

991 Nogee, Philip, and Levin, Murray B. "Some Determi-
     nants of Political Attitudes Among College Voters."
     Public Opinion Quarterly 22 (winter 1958): 449-463.

992 Nolan, W. A. "What Can Women Do? Opportunities
     for Assuming Political Roles." Social Order 3 (Sep-
     tember 1953): 301-304.

993 "Non-Partisan Way to be Involved in Politics." Good
     Housekeeping 174 (June 1972): 169.

994 "No Votes for Women." Time 57 (12 March 1951): 32.

995 "Now It's Seventeen Women in Congress." U.S. News
     and World Report 45 (12 December 1958): 80.

996 "Now Women Talk Back." Life 72 (9 June 1972): 46-50.

997 "Number One Method." Nation 210 (26 January 1970):
     69-70.

998 "N.W.P.C. Has a Running Start on 1972." Spokes-
     woman (1 November 1971): 6.

999 "NWPC Launches 'Win With Women '74'." Spokes-
     woman 4 (15 April 1974): 3.

1000 Olivier, W. "League of Frightened Women." Saturday
     Evening Post 227 (23 October 1954): 32-33.

1001 "158 Women Serving as Mayors or Governing Body
     Members in New Jersey's Local Governments."
     New Jersey Municipalities 51 (June 1974): 12-13.

1002 O'Neill, William L. "Feminism as a Radical Ideol-
     ogy." In The Underside of American History:
     Other Readings, vol. 2, edited by Thomas R.
     Frazier. New York: Harcourt, Brace, Jovano-
     vich, 1971.

1003 Oppenheimer, Valerie D. "Demographic Influence on
     Female Employment and Status of Women."
     American Journal of Sociology 78 (January 1973):
     946-961.

1004 Orcutt, James. "The Impact of Student Activism on
     Attitudes Toward the Female Sex Role." Social
     Forces 54 (December 1975): 387.

1005 Ortner, Sherry B. "Is Female to Male as Nature is
     to Culture?" Feminist Studies 1 (fall 1972): 5-32.

1006 Orum, Anthony, et al. "Sex, Socialization and Poli-
     tics." American Sociological Review 39 (April
     1974): 197-209.

1007 "Our Miss Brooks: Chairman of United Nation's
     Fourth Trusteeship Committee." Ebony 17 (Decem-
     ber 1961): 122-124.

1008 "The Outsiders on the Inside." Newsweek 80 (24
     July 1972): 32.

1009 "Pa and Ma Wallace as a Dynasty." Life 60 (11
     March 1966): 4.

1010 Paizis, Suzanne. "Frustrated Majority: Conscious-
     ness-Raising at the Ballot Box." California
     Journal: The Monthly Report on State Government
     and Politics (March 1974): 80-83.

1011 Palmer, H. "Our Votes Can Help Shape the Destiny
     of Nations." Independent Woman 33 (October 1954):
     382.

1012 Papachristou, Judith. "Women's Christian Temperance
     Union: Fighting More and Demon Rum." Ms. 4
     (June 1976): 73.

1013   Parish, A. "Political Role of Women in America."
       Phi Delta Delta 35 (June 1957): 12.

1014   Patterson, Sue McCauley. "Political Update: From
       Maryland with Promise (and Reservations)." Ms.
       3 (April 1975): 77-80.

1015   Pawlicki, Robert, and Almquist, Carol. "Authori-
       tarianism, Locus of Control and Tolerance of Am-
       biguity as Reflected in Membership and Nonmember-
       ship in a Women's Liberation Group." Psychologi-
       cal Reports 32 (June 1973): 1331-1337.

1016   Payne, J. W. "Women, Man Your Stations." Ameri-
       can Mercury 78 (January 1954): 83-86.

1017   Peterson, Esther. "Mrs. Roosevelt's Legacy: Report
       on the Status of Women." McCalls 91 (October
       1963): 84.

1018   "Petticoat Rule in New Mexico." Life 28 (29 May
       1950): 24-25.

1019   Pheterson, G. I.; Kresler, S. B.; and Goldberg, P. A.
       "Evaluation of the Performance of Women as a
       Function of Their Sex, Achievement, and Personal
       History." Journal of Personality and Social Psy-
       chology 19 (1971): 114-118.

1020   Phillips, B. J. "Recognizing the Gentleladies of the
       Judiciary Committee." Ms. 3 (November 1974):
       70-74.

1021   Pierce, B. "What Do Women Want at the Conven-
       tions?" McCalls 99 (July 1972): 42.

1022   Pierce, John C.; Avery, William P.; and Carey,
       Addison, Jr. "Sex Differences in Black Political
       Beliefs and Behavior." American Journal of
       Political Science 17 (May 1973): 422-430.

1023   "Political Clubs for Women Only." Good Housekeeping
       146 (February 1958): 131-132.

1024   "Politics Is Women's Work." Economist 241 (23 Octo-
       ber 1971): 51.

1025   Polk, Barbara Bovee. "Male Power and the Women's

Movement." Journal of Applied Behavioral Science
10 (1974): 415-431.

1026 _____ . "Women's Liberation: Movement for
Equality." In Toward a Sociology of Women,
edited by Constantina Safilios-Rothschild. Lexington, Mass.: Xerox College, 1972.

1027 Pollitzer, A. "Her Honor, the Judge, B. S. Matthews,
U.S. District Court for the District of Colombia."
Independent Woman 30 (January 1951): 11-12.

1028 Poppy, J. "Politics on the Split Level Frontier:
Jocelyn Marchisio from Seattle." Look 31 (16
May 1967): 94.

1029 Porter, Mary, and Matasar, Ann B. "The Role and
Status of Women in the Daley Organization." In
Women in Politics, edited by Jane S. Jaquette.
New York: John Wiley, 1974.

1030 "Power of Woman." Ladies Home Journal 87 (April
1970): 82.

1031 "President's Project Launched; Register of Women in
Government." National Business Woman 29
(February 1960): 21.

1032 Prestage, Jewel. "Black Women Officeholders: The
Case of State Legislators." In Women in the Professions, edited by Laurily Keir Epstein. Lexington, Mass.: D. C. Heath, Lexington Books, 1975.

1033 Price, Colette. "The Feminist Party." Woman's
World (March/April/May 1972): 2.

1034 Priest, I. B. "Ladies Elected Ike." American
Mercury 76 (February 1953): 23-28.

1035 Priestley, John Boynton. "Speaking Out: Women Don't
Run the Country." Saturday Evening Post 237 (12
December 1967): 8.

1036 Prindle, Janice. "Women Legislators: A Paradox of
Power." Empire State Report 2 (January/February
1976): 3.

1037 Pringle, H. F., and Pringle, K. "He Followed Mom

to Congress." Saturday Evening Post 226 (15 August 1953): 25.

1038 "Progress Report on Women in Government Policy Making Posts." Independent Woman 33 (January 1954): 4.

1039 Ratcliff, J. D. "Justice: Edith Sampson Style." Reader's Digest 93 (November 1968): 167.

1040 Ratdorff, V. R. "Hard Work: She Likes It." Independent Woman 32 (December 1953): 441-442.

1041 Rath, J. Arthur. "Women as Community Leaders: And How They Exercise Their Role in A Typical City--A Survey Report." Public Relations Journal 27 (January 1971): 19-20.

1042 "Record High for Women in Congress." Independent Woman 33 (December 1954): 458.

1043 Reeves, Richard. "The City Politic: The Woman Thing." New York 5 (14 February 1972): 8-9.

1044 Reid, E. E. "Ladies Run Clerk's Office in 91 Cities." Alabama Municipal Journal (September 1954): 7-9.

1045 Remmers, H. H. "Early Socialization of Attitudes." In American Voting Behavior, edited by Eugene Burdick and Arthur J. Brodbeck. Glencoe, Ill.: Free Press, 1959.

1046 "Republican Delegates: Representation Being Widened." Congressional Quarterly Weekly Report (12 August 1972): 1998-1999.

1047 Rhea, Daniel F. B. "Political Power for Women." Survey of Business, The University of Tennessee 10 (May/June 1975): 21.

1048 "Right Decision: Exclusion of Male Members." Nation 214 (22 May 1974): 645.

1049 Rixey, L. "Mrs. Smith Really Goes to Town." Colliers 126 (29 July 1950): 20-21.

1050 Robertson, Mary Helen. "Constitutional Revision in

Illinois: The League of Women Voters Role."
National Civic Review 60 (September 1971): 438-
443.

1051 Robinson, Donald. "America's Seventy-Five Most Important Women." _Ladies Home Journal_ (January
1971): 71-73.

1052 Rokeach, Milton. "Change and Stability in American
Value Systems, 1968-1971." _Public Opinion
Quarterly_ 38 (summer 1974): 222-238.

1053 Romney, Lenore. "Men, Women and Politics." _Look_
35 (6 April 1971): 11.

1054 Rose, Arnold. "The Adequacy of Women's Expectations for Adult Roles." _Social Forces_ 30 (October
1951): 69-77.

1055 Rose, Deborah. "Lookin' Around: How Women Are
Regaining Control." _Second Wave_ 2 (1973): 23-24.

1056 Rosenberg, Morris. "Some Determinants of Political
Apathy." _Public Opinion Quarterly_ 18 (winter
1954): 349-366.

1057 Rosenfeld, Raymond A. "Membership Characteristics
of Voluntary Organizations: Two Groups Involved
in Atlanta School Desegregation." _Journal of the
Georgia Political Science Association_ 1 (fall 1972):
77-99.

1058 Rossi, Alice S. "Equality between the Sexes: An Im-
modest Proposal." _Daedalus_ 93 (spring 1964):
607-652.

1059 _____. "Women--Terms of Liberation." _Dissent_
(November/December 1970): 531-541.

1060 Rostow, Edna. "Conflict and Accommodation."
Daedalus 93 (spring 1964): 735-760.

1061 Ruether, Rosemary Radford. "Women's Liberation,
Ecology, and Social Revolution." _WIN_ 9 (11
October 1973): 4-7.

1062 "Running and Hoping: Some of Our November Candidates." _Ms._ 3 (October 1974): 115-118.

1063 Ryan, J. E. "Does Justice Have Gender?" *America*
      118 (23 March 1968): 375-377.

1064 Sadler, C. "Women Behind Ike." *McCalls* 80 (April
      1953): 52-53.

1065 Salisbury, Robert. "The Urban Party Organization
      Member." *Public Opinion Quarterly* 29 (winter
      1965): 550-564.

1066 Sallach, David L.; Babchuk, Nicholas; and Booth, Alan.
      "Social Involvement and Political Activity: Another
      View." *Social Science Quarterly* 52 (March 1972):
      879-892.

1067 Salper, Roberta. "The Theory and Practice of Wo-
      men's Studies." *Edcentric* 3 (December 1971): 4-8.

1068 "Salute to the Women of the 89th Congress." *National
      Business Woman* 44 (January 1965): 25-28.

1069 "Salute to Women in Politics." *Independent Woman* 34
      (March 1955): 104.

1070 Samuels, Gertrude. "Really a Man's World, Politics."
      New York Times Magazine (15 October 1950): 17.

1071 Sanders, Elizabeth Braly. "What Do Young Women
      Want?" *Youth and Society* 3 (September 1971):
      36-59.

1072 Sanders, Marian K. "Issues Girls, Club Ladies, Camp
      Followers." *New York Times Magazine* (1 Decem-
      ber 1963): 38.

1073 _____. "Women in Politics." *Harpers* 211 (August
      1955): 20.

1074 Sandy, Peggy R. "Female Status in the Public Domain."
      In *Woman, Culture and Society*, edited by Michelle
      Rosaldo and Louise Lamphere. Stanford, Calif.:
      Stanford University Press, 1974.

1075 Sassower, Doris L. "The Legal Rights of Professional
      Women." *Contemporary Education* 43 (February
      1972): 205-208.

1076   Schneir, Miriam.   "The Woman Who Ran for President
       in 1872."   Ms. 1 (September 1972): 84-89.

1077   Schwindt, H. D.   "This Beautiful Force: First Na-
       tional Convention."   Newsweek 81 (26 February
       1973): 31-32.

1078   Scott, Anne Firor.   "After Suffrage: Southern Women
       in the '20's."   Journal of Southern History 30
       (August 1964): 298-318.

1079   _____ .   "Feminism vs. the Feds."   Issues in
       Industrial Society 2 (1971): 32-46.

1080   _____ .   "Jane Addams and the City."   Virginia
       Quarterly Review 43 (winter 1967): 53-62.

1081   _____ .   "The 'New Women' in the New South."
       South Atlantic Quarterly 61 (fall 1962).

1082   Scott, Bonnie K.   "Pedestal or Gallery: A Literary
       Perspective of Woman's Role in Politics."   In The
       Role of Women in Politics, edited by Mae R.
       Carter.   Newark, Del.:   University of Delaware,
       Division of Continuing Education, 1964.

1083   Scott, John C., Jr.   "Membership and Participation
       in Voluntary Associations."   American Sociological
       Review 22 (June 1957): 315-326.

1084   Seifer, Nancy.   "Barbara Mikulski and the Blue-Collar
       Women."   Ms. 2 (November 1973): 70-74.

1085   Setlow, Carolyn, and Steinem, Gloria.   "Why Women
       Voted for Richard Nixon."   Ms. 1 (March 1973): 66.

1086   "Sexism - Part of National Platform of People's Party
       1974 Convention, Indianapolis, Indiana, July 4-6,
       1974."   Grass Roots (April 1974): 14.

1087   Shaffer, Helen B.   "Status of Women."   Congressional
       Quarterly Editorial Research Reports 2 (5 August
       1970): 565-585.

1088   _____ .   "Women in Politics."   Congressional
       Quarterly Editorial Research Reports (20 February
       1956): 119-136.

1089   Shallet, Sidney. "Is There a Woman's Vote?" Satur-
       day Evening Post 233 (17 September 1960): 31.

1090   Shanley, Mary L., and Schuck, Victoria. "In Search
       of Political Woman." Social Science Quarterly 55
       (December 1974): 632-644.

1091   Shear, S. Sue. "The 27th in Missouri." FOCUS/Mid-
       west 9 (1973): 21.

1092   Shearer, Lloyd, and Dunlap, Carol. "The First Wo-
       man President of the U.S.--Why Not and When?"
       Parade (7 February 1971): 4-6.

1093   Sherr, Lynn. "Democratic Women." Saturday Review
       (5 August 1972): 6-8.

1094   Shilvock, A. R., and Schnepp, G. J. "Women in Poli-
       tics: Catholic Collegiate Attitudes." Social Order
       3 (October 1953): 361-366.

1095   Sigelman, Lee. "The Curious Case of Women in State
       and Local Government." Social Science Quarterly
       56 (March 1976): 591-604.

1096   Simms, Madeleine. "Abortion Politics in New York."
       New Scientist 57 (1 February 1973): 252-253.

1097   Sipilä, H. L. "Women and World Affairs." Today's
       Education 63 (November 1974): 66-67.

1098   "Sisters of Abigail Adams." Time 55 (6 February
       1950): 12-13.

1099   Slater, Carol. "Class Differences in Definition of
       Role and Membership in Voluntary Associations
       Among Urban Women." American Journal of
       Sociology 65 (1961): 616-659.

1100   Slater, L. "Woman's Suffrage." McCalls 88 (Septem-
       ber 1961): 84-93.

1101   Sloan, Margaret, and Steinem, Gloria. "Ms: Today
       and Tomorrow." Civil Rights Digest 5 (spring
       1973): 35-42.

1102   Smith, James Howell. "Mrs. Ben Hooper of Oshkosh:

Peace Worker and Politician." Wisconsin Magazine of History 36 (winter 1962-63): 124-135.

1103 Smith, L. "Gloria Steinem, Writer and Social Critic, Talks About Sex, Politics, and Marriage." Redbook 138 (January 1972): 68-76.

1104 Smith, Leticia. "Women as Volunteers: The Double Subsidy." Journal of Voluntary Action Research 4 (summer/fall 1975): 119-136.

1105 Smith, M. G. "What a Political Club Can Do for You." Independent Woman 33 (February 1954): 57-58.

1106 Smith, Marion. "Women in Pennsylvania Local Government." Pennsylvanian (May 1976): 6-8.

1107 Smith, Robert G. "Three Women Leaders Beset by Problems." U.S. News and World Report 70 (10 May 1971): 42.

1108 "Something for the Girls; President Johnson Appoints Women to Ten Government Posts." Newsweek 63 (16 March 1964): 29-30.

1109 Sorenson, T. C. "Special Report on the Woman Voter." Redbook 130 (April 1968): 61.

1110 Stein, A., and Smithells, J. "Age and Sex Differences in Children's Sex Role Standards About Achievement." Developmental Psychology 1 (1969): 252-259.

1111 Steinem, Gloria. "After Black Power, Women's Liberation." New York (7 April 1969): 8-10.

1112 _____. "Coming of Age with McGovern." Ms. 1 (October 1972): 39.

1113 _____, et al. "Special Section: Running for Office ... How to Campaign on the Issues, Lobby for Your Interests, and Reform Your Party and the System Itself." Ms. 2 (April 1974): 61-68.

1114 _____. "The Ticket that Might Have Been: President Chisholm." Ms. 1 (January 1973): 72-74.

1115 _____ . "Why We Need a Woman President in
        1976." Look 34 (13 January 1970): 58.

1116 _____ . "Women Voters Can't Be Trusted." Ms.
        1 (July 1972): 47.

1117 Steininger, Marion, and Lesser, Harvey. "Sex and
        Generation Differences and Similarity in Social Atti-
        tudes." Journal of Consulting Psychology 21 (1974):
        459-460.

1118 Stern, L. "Housewife in Politics." American Maga-
        zine 158 (October 1954): 22-25.

1119 Stewart, Alva. "Feminine City Managers." American
        City 79 (May 1964): 154.

1120 _____ . "Why, When and How of Women Mayors."
        American City 83 (September 1968): 168.

1121 _____ . "Women in City Management." Municipal
        South 10 (January 1963): 20-22.

1122 Stoloff, Carolyn. "Who Joins Women's Liberation?"
        Psychiatry 36 (August 1973): 325-340.

1123 Stowe, L. "Eugenie Anderson Shows the Flag."
        Reader's Digest 86 (March 1965): 173.

1124 Streijffert, Helena. "The Women's Movement: A
        Theoretical Discussion." Acta Sociologica 17
        (1974): 344-366.

1125 Strodtbeck, Fred L.; Bezdek, William; and Goldhamer,
        Don. "Male Sex-Role and Response to a Community
        Problem." Sociological Quarterly 11 (summer
        1970): 291-306.

1126 Strum, Philippa. "The Supreme Court and Sexual
        Equality: A Cast Study of Factors Affecting Judicial
        Policy-Making." Policy Studies Journal 4 (winter
        1975): 146-150.

1127 Stuart, Julia D. "Women Carry the Day." National
        Municipal Review (now National Civic Review) 46
        (February 1957): 66-70.

1128 Stuart, Mrs. Robert J. "New Political Power of Wo-
     men." Ladies Home Journal 81 (September 1964):
     68.

1129 Stucker, John J. "Women as Voters: Their Matura-
     tion as Political Persons in American Society."
     In Women in the Professions, edited by Laurily
     Keir Epstein. Lexington, Mass.: D. C. Heath,
     Lexington Books, 1975.

1130 Summerskill, Shirley. "United Women." Contemporary
     Review (November 1971): 225-229.

1131 "Susan B. Anthony Elected to Hall of Fame." Inde-
     pendent Woman 29 (December 1950): 379.

1132 "Susan B. Anthony Placed in Hall of Fame." Inde-
     pendent Woman 31 (June 1952): 165-166.

1133 Tavris, Carol. "Who Likes Women's Lib and Why:
     The Case of the Unliberated Liberals." Journal
     of Social Issues 29:4 (1973): 175-198.

1134 Taylor, Suzanne S. "Educational Leadership: A
     Male Domain?" Phi Delta Kappan 55 (October
     1973): 124-128.

1135 Temple, M. L. "What Do Our Congressmen Think
     About the Equal Rights Amendment?" Independent
     Woman 32 (April 1953): 127.

1136 _____. "Women in the 83rd Congress." Inde-
     pendent Woman 32 (February 1953): 34-36.

1137 "These Groups Have Led the Way...." AAUW Journal
     69 (November 1975): 21.

1138 "They Do It, You Can Too; Wives and Mothers in Our
     State Legislatures." Ladies Home Journal 73
     (April 1956): 70-71.

1139 "They Liked Mike: Republican Women's National
     Conference." Reporter 18 (3 April 1958): 2.

1140 "This Mayor Is Sister." American City 85 (December
     1970): 51.

1141 Thompson, Marian. "Equal Rights for Women in the
      Public Schools." In Meeting the Challenges of
      School Board Leadership: The Report of the NSBA
      Summer Institute at Dartmouth College, August 14-
      18, 1972. Evanston, Ill.: National School Boards
      Association, 1973.

1142 Thornburgh, Margaret. "Women and Elections."
      American Federationist 62 (March 1955): 16-18.

1143 Thorne, Barrie. "Women in the Draft Resistance
      Movement: A Case Study of Sex Roles and Social
      Movements." Sex Roles 1 (June 1975): 179.

1144 Thumin, Fred J. "The Relation of Liberalism to Sex,
      Age, Academic Field and College Grades." Journal
      of Clinical Psychology 28 (April 1972): 160-164.

1145 Timms, Duncan W. G., and Timms, Elizabeth A.
      "Anomie and Social Participation Among Suburban
      Women." Pacific Sociological Review 15 (January
      1972): 123-142.

1146 Tinker, Irene. "Nonacademic Professional Political
      Scientists." American Behavioral Scientist (Decem-
      ber 1971): 206-212.

1147 Tolchin, Susan, and Tolchin, Martin. "Getting Clout."
      Esquire 80 (July 1973): 112-115.

1148 Tormey, Judith. "The Morality of Self-Sacrifice and
      the History of Feminism." In The Role of Women
      in Politics, edited by Mae R. Carter. Newark,
      Del.: University of Delaware, Division of Con-
      tinuing Education, 1964.

1149 "Toward Female Power at the Poles." Time 99 (20
      March 1972): 33-34.

1150 "To Wear Mantle of India Edwards: Mrs. Walter
      Louchheim." Independent Woman 32 (November
      1953): 40.

1151 Treaster, Joseph B. "Ella Grasso of Connecticut:
      Running and Winning." Ms. 3 (October 1974): 80.

1152 Trecker, J. L. "Suffrage Prisoner." American
      Scholar 41 (summer 1972): 409-423.

1153 Trepte, E. H. "No New Thing Under the Sun." Independent Woman 35 (October 1956): 6.

1154 "Tribute to Our Women in Congress." Independent Woman 34 (February 1955): 48-50.

1155 Tucker, C. Delores. "The Black Woman in Politics. In Extension of Remarks of Donald M. Fraser." Congressional Record 121 (4 June 1975): E2854-E2855.

1156 UNESCO. "Images of Women in Society." Institute of Social Sciences Journal 14 (1962): 7-70.

1157 "The United Nations and the Status of Women." United Nations Review 8 (March 1961): 22-27.

1158 U.S., Congress, Senate, Subcommittee on Reports, Accounting, and Management. "Discrimination Against Women and Blacks in Federal Advisory Committee Appointments." Congressional Record (17 September 1976): S16073.

1159 Vaughan, Donald S. "Women in Mississippi Government." Public Administration Survey 9 (May 1962): 1-4.

1160 "Vermont Ladies Are Taking Over; Members of Legislature." Life 34 (6 April 1953): 21-23.

1161 Viorst, Judith. "Congresswoman Pat Schroeder: The Woman Who Has a Bear By the Tail." Redbook (November 1973): 97.

1162 Virden, H. "Knock on Every Door." Independent Woman 31 (October 1952): 303.

1163 "Virginia Elects All-Woman Slate." American City 65 (September 1950): 153.

1164 Volgy, Thomas J., and Volgy, Sandra Sue. "Women and Politics: Political Correlates of Sex-Role Acceptance." Social Science Quarterly 55 (March 1975): 967-974.

1165 Wakefield, D. "Outsiders." Esquire 58 (July 1962): 91-93.

1166 Walter, Lowe M., and Marzolf, Stanley. "The Relation
      of Sex, Age, and School Achievement to Levels of
      Aspiration." Journal of Educational Psychology 42
      (1951): 285-292.

1167 Walters, Robert. "The Year of the Woman?" National
      Journal Reports 6 (2 November 1974): 1660.

1168 Weinberg, Barbara. "Political Action in AAUW:
      More than a Choice." AAUW Journal 69 (Novem-
      ber 1975): 11-13.

1169 Weir, E. T. "Can You Afford to Stay Out of Politics?"
      Independent Woman 31 (February 1952): 33.

1170 Weis, Jessica M. "Organizing the Women." In Poli-
      tics, U.S.A.: A Practical Guide to the Winning of
      Public Office, edited by James Cannon. New York:
      Doubleday, 1960.

1171 Weiss, Robert S., and Samuelson, Nancy M. "Special
      Roles of American Women." Journal of Marriage
      and the Family 20 (November 1958): 358-366.

1172 Weitzman, Lenore J. "Sex-Role Socialization." In
      Women: A Feminist Perspective, edited by Jo
      Freeman. Palo Alto, Calif.: Mayfield, 1974.

1173 Wells, Audrey Siess, and Smeal, Eleanor. "Women's
      Attitudes Toward Women in Politics: A Survey of
      Urban Registered Voters and Party Committee-
      women." In Women in Politics, edited by Jane S.
      Jaquette. New York: John Wiley, 1974.

1174 Werner, Emmy. "Women in Congress: 1917-1964."
      Western Political Quarterly 19 (March 1966): 16-30.

1175 _____. "Women in State Legislatures." Western
      Political Quarterly 21 (March 1968): 40-50.

1176 _____, and Bachtold, Louise M. "Personality
      Characteristics of Women in American Politics."
      In Women in Politics, edited by Jane S. Jaquette.
      New York: John Wiley, 1974.

1177 Westoff, Leslie Aldridge. "Is a Women's Revolution
      Really Possible? Yes." McCalls (October 1969): 76.

1178 Weston, Marybeth. "Ladies' Day on the Hustings."
      New York Times Magazine (19 October 1958): 32.

1179 "What Women Did in Gary." Ladies Home Journal
      68 (October 1951): 51.

1180 "What Women Do In Politics: Interviews with the Two
      Women Leaders of the Republican and Democratic
      Parties." U.S. News and World Report 45 (12
      December 1958): 72-79.

1181 "When a Mom Goes into Politics: Mrs. Knutson."
      U.S. News and World Report 45 (5 September 1958):
      42-43.

1182 "When a Woman Runs the Town." Ladies Home
      Journal 69 (January 1952): 49.

1183 "When the Women Struck for Equality." U.S. News
      and World Report (7 September 1970): 26.

1184 "Where She Is and Where She's Going." Time 90
      (20 March 1972): 26-28.

1185 White, Jean Bickmore. "Gentle Persuaders: Utah's
      First Women Legislators." Utah Historical Quar-
      terly 38 (winter 1970): 31-49.

1186 White, Mary L. "Mary White: Autobiography of an
      Ohio First Lady." Ohio History 82 (winter/spring
      1973): 63-87.

1187 White, William S. "Public Women." Harpers 220
      (January 1960): 86-88.

1188 Whitton, Mary O. "At Home with Lucretia Mott."
      American Scholar 20 (spring 1951): 175-184.

1189 "Who's Come a Long Way, Baby?" Time (31 August
      1976): 16-21.

1190 "Who's New in Congress." Time 97 (1 February
      1971): 15.

1191 Wiener, Rosalind. "How a Woman Member of a City
      Council Sees Her Job." American City 69 (April
      1954): 119.

1192/3　Wilkinson, Sandra. "Women in Government: The Role of Women as Members of Local Governing Bodies." Virginia Town and City (April 1974): 18-19.

1194　Williams, Roger M. "Fighting City Hall: The Rise of Middle Class Activism." Saturday Review (March 1975): 12-16.

1195　"Will Women Decide the Election?" U.S. News and World Report 49 (3 October 1960): 61-65.

1196　"Wives on Campaign Trail Wave Good-Bye to Tradition." U.S. News and World Report (7 June 1976): 18-19.

1197　Wohl, Lisa Cronin. "Phyllis Schlafly: 'The Sweetheart of the Silent Majority.'" Ms. (March 1974): 55-57.

1198　Wolfe, Deborah P. "Black Women in Politics." AAUW Journal 69 (November 1975): 19.

1199　"A Woman for President? Hurdles in the Path of Margaret Chase Smith." U.S. News and World Report 56 (10 February 1964): 34-36.

1200　"Woman of Courage." Ebony 16 (April 1961): 70-72.

1201　"Woman's Dilemma--Home or Politics: Getting Elected Is Just One Problem for Office-Holding Wife." U.S. News and World Report 44 (23 May 1958): 68-70.

1202　"Woman's Place." Atlantic Monthly 225 (March 1970): 82-126.

1203　"A Woman's Place Is in the House." National Voter 22 (March/April 1972): 1-5.

1204　"Woman Voters Have Made Our Politics Very, Very Different." Saturday Evening Post 233 (27 August 1960): 10.

1205　"Woman with the Fighting Heart." Independent Woman 33 (February 1954): 55-56.

1206 "Women Around the World." Center Magazine 7 (May/ June 1974): 43-80.

1207 "Women Attend Crash Course on Delegate Selection." Spokeswoman (1 April 1972): 2.

1208 "Women Candidates: A Big Increase over 1972." Congressional Quarterly Weekly Report 32 (26 October 1974): 2973-2974.

1209 "Women Candidates: Many More Predicted for 1974." Congressional Quarterly Weekly Report 32 (13 April 1974): 941-944.

1210 "Women in Congress Now Number Eleven." Independent Woman 30 (October 1951): 311.

1211 "Women in Government." Public Management 55 (February 1973): see entire issue.

1212 "Women in Government: Interviews with 6 in Top Jobs." U.S. News and World Report 72 (17 January 1972): 62-69.

1213 "Women in History: A Re-Creation of Our Past." Women: A Journal of Liberation 1 (spring 1970): see entire issue.

1214 "Women in Municipal Government." Maine Townsman (July 1973).

1215 "Women in Office: Foretaste of the Future." Nation's Business 63 (April 1975): 26-31.

1216 "Women in Politics." Ladies Home Journal 68 (November 1951): 25.

1217 "Women in Politics." Women in America: The Gallup Opinion Index 128 (March 1976): 2-16.

1218 "Women in Politics." Women's Agenda 1 (April 1976): see entire issue.

1219 "Women in Politics and Business." America 90 (14 November 1953): 162.

1220 "Women in Politics: An Interview with Edith Green." Social Policy (January/February 1972): 16-22.

1221 "Women in Politics: Catholic Collegiate Attitudes."
Social Order 3 (October 1953): 361-366.

1222 "Women in Politics: Leading Candidates in 1970,
Their Election Prospects, Past and Present Members." Congressional Quarterly Weekly Report 28
(10 July 1970): 1745-1748.

1223 "Women in Public Office Tell Us More." Independent
Woman 29 (November 1950): 341-342.

1224 "Women in the 84th Congress." Independent Woman
34 (January 1955): 20-23.

1225 "Women in Trade Unions." Labour Gazette 71 (October
1971): 682-685.

1226 "Women: Make Policy Not Coffee." National Voter
(January/February 1972): 1-4.

1227 "Women Office Holders Talk of Their Campaigns....
Their Work....Their Hopes." AAUW Journal 69
(November 1975): 14.

1228 "Women Office-Seekers: This Year, More Than Ever."
Congressional Quarterly Weekly Report 30 (28
October 1972): 2800.

1229 "Women of Rotzo: Mayor and Town Council." Newsweek 65 (12 April 1965): 52.

1230 "Women of the Year." Time (20 March 1972): 6-22.

1231 "Women's Place Is--In Politics." Congressional Quarterly Weekly Report 11 (6 November 1953): 1308-
1309.

1232 "'Women's Political Caucus'--What It Is, What It
Wants." U.S. News and World Report 71 (16
August 1971): 67-68.

1233 "Women Unite." Leviathan 2 (May 1970): see entire
issue.

1234 "Women Who Make State Laws; Negro Women Holding
State Legislative Posts." Ebony 22 (September
1967): 27-30.

1235 "Women You'd Like to Know." Farm Journal 94
      (May 1970): 60-61.

1236 Worden, Helen. "Pretty Good Politician." Colliers
      125 (14 January 1950): 18-19.

1237 Wright, Betsey. "Women Can Win: How to Plan and
      Run an Effective Campaign." AAUW Journal 69
      (November 1975): 7-10.

1238 "The Year of the Woman." Newsweek (4 November
      1974): 20-27.

1239 Young, Louise M. "The American Woman at Mid-
      Century." American Review 2 (December 1961):
      121-138.

1240 Zikmund, Joseph, and Smith, Robert. "Political
      Participation in an Upper-Middle-Class Suburb."
      Urban Affairs Quarterly 4 (June 1969): 443-458.

1241 Zikmund, William G., and Miller, Stephen J. "In-
      ternal-External Control of Reinforcement and Wo-
      men's Participation in Direct Social Action."
      Psychology Reports 34 (June 1974): 1163-1166.

DISSERTATIONS AND THESES

1242 Almanzor, Angelina C. "Volunteer and Staff Participation in a Voluntary Social Welfare Association in the United States: A Study of the National Young Women's Christian Association." D.S.W. dissertation, Columbia University, 1961.

1243 Axelrod, Morris. "A Study of Formal and Informal Group Participation in a Large Urban Community." Ph.D. dissertation, University of Michigan, 1953.

1244 Banthin, Joanne Marie. "The New York State Women's Political Caucus: A Case Study in Organizational Behavior." Ph.D. dissertation, University of Michigan, 1973.

1245 Bauer, Constance. "Voluntary Associations among Women of Two Classes in Urban Colorado." Ph.D. dissertation, University of Colorado, 1975.

1246 Berry, Frankye. "Survey of a Selected Number of Women's Organizations in Tampa, Florida and Their Contributions to Education." Ed.D. dissertation, University of Florida, 1975.

1247 Blahna, Loretta J. "The Rhetoric of the Equal Rights Amendment." Ph.D. dissertation, University of Kansas, 1973.

1248 Booth, Alan. "Personal Influence on the Decision to Join Voluntary Associations." Ph.D. dissertation, University of Nebraska, 1970.

1249 Brehm, Barbara. "American Women Judges." Master's thesis, Michigan State University, 1974.

1250 Buckman, Relma. "Interaction between Women's Clubs and Institutions in Greater Lafayette, Indiana." Ph.D. dissertation, University of Chicago, 1953.

1251 Burrell, Barbara. "A New Dimension in Political
      Participation: The Women's Political Caucus."
      Master's thesis, Iowa State University, 1975.

1252 Carroll, Susan. "Women's Rights and Political
      Parties: Issue Development, the 1972 Conventions,
      and the National Women's Political Caucus."
      Master's thesis, Indiana University, 1975.

1253 Cassell, Joan. "A Group Called Women: Recruitment
      and Organization in Contemporary American Femi-
      nism." Ph.D. dissertation, Columbia University,
      1975.

1254 Chafe, William. "From Suffrage to Liberation: The
      Changing Role of American Women, 1920-1970."
      Ph.D. dissertation, Columbia University, 1971.

1255 Cowan, Margie Louise. "Personality Factors in Wo-
      men Affecting Their Degree of Political Involve-
      ment." Ph.D. dissertation, Oklahoma State Uni-
      versity, 1974.

1256 Crigler, Patricia Woodall. "Significant Variables
      Indicative of Commitment to the Women's Move-
      ment." Ph.D. dissertation, Northwestern Uni-
      versity, 1973.

1257 Dennison, Laura. "Political Participation of American
      Women: Effects of Sex Stereotypes and Political
      Socialization." Master's thesis, Claremont Graduate
      School, 1973.

1258 Diamond, Irene. "Women and the State Legislatures:
      A Macro and Micro Analysis." Ph.D. dissertation,
      Princeton University, 1975.

1259 Doyle, William T. "Charlotte Perkins Gilman and the
      Cycle of Feminist Reform." Ph.D. dissertation,
      University of California, 1960.

1260 Elshtain, Jean Bethke. "Women and Politics: A
      Theoretical Analysis." Ph.D. dissertation, Brandeis
      University, 1973.

1261 Feagans, Janet. "Female Political Elites: Case
      Studies of Female Legislators." Ph.D. disserta-
      tion, Howard University, 1972.

1262 Fletty, Valborg Esther. "Public Services of Women's
      Organizations." Ph. D. dissertation, Syracuse
      University, 1952.

1263 Freeman, Bonnie Cook. "A New Political Woman."
      Ph. D. dissertation, University of Wisconsin, 1975.

1264 Freeman, Jo. "The Politics of Women's Liberation:
      A Case Study of an Emerging Social Movement in
      its Relation to the Policy Process." Ph. D. disser-
      tation, University of Chicago, 1973.

1265 Gardner, Mary E. "The Negro Woman: Her Role as
      Participant in Volunteer Community Activities in
      Westchester Communities." Ed. D. dissertation,
      New York University, 1961.

1266 Gehlen, Frieda L. "Role Stress and Cultural Resources:
      A Study of the Role of the Woman Member of Con-
      gress." Ph. D. dissertation, Michigan State Uni-
      versity, 1967.

1267 Gouldner, Helen P. "The Organization Woman: Pat-
      terns of Friendship and Organization Commitment."
      Ph. D. dissertation, University of California at Los
      Angeles, 1960.

1268 Gusfield, Joseph R. "Organizational Change: A Study
      of the Women's Christian Temperance Union."
      Ph. D. dissertation, University of Chicago, 1955.

1269 Harris, Ted Charlton. "Jeannette Rankin: Suffragist,
      First Woman Elected to Congress, and a Pacifist."
      Ph. D. dissertation, University of Georgia, 1972.

1270 Hurwitz, Mark William. "The Personal Characteristics
      and Attitudes of New Jersey School Board Members."
      Ph. D. dissertation, Temple University, 1971.

1271 Johnson, Dorothy E. "Organized Women and National
      Legislation: 1920-1941." Ph. D. dissertation,
      Western Reserve University, 1960.

1272 Johnson, Lillian. "The Role Orientation of Women in
      Voluntary Associations in Raleigh, North Carolina."
      Ph. D. dissertation, North Carolina State Univer-
      sity, 1972.

1273   Josephson, Clifford R.   "Composition and Other
       Characteristics of Voluntary Boards." Ed. D. dis-
       sertation, Cornell University, 1963.

1274   Kruschke, Earl Rogers.   "Female Politicals and
       Apoliticals: Some Measurements and Comparisons."
       Ph. D. dissertation, University of Wisconsin, 1963.

1275   Kunkle, Debora Ellen.   "Women and Politics: The
       Political Role Expectations of Adolescent Females."
       Ph. D. dissertation, State University of New York
       at Buffalo, 1974.

1276   Kyle, Patricia A.   "Political Sex-Role Distinctions:
       Motivations, Recruitment and Demography of Wo-
       men Party Elites in North Carolina." Ph. D. dis-
       sertation, Georgetown University, 1973.

1277   Lansing, Marjorie.   "Sex Differences in Political Par-
       ticipation." Ph. D. dissertation, University of
       Michigan, 1971.

1278   Lee, Marcia Manning.   "The Participation of Women
       in Suburban Politics: A Study of the Influence of
       Women As Compared to Men in Suburban Govern-
       mental Decision-Making." Ph. D. dissertation,
       Tufts University, 1973.

1279   Lemons, James Stanley.   "The New Woman from the
       Great War to the Great Depression." Ph. D. dis-
       sertation, University of Missouri, 1967.

1280   Levitt, Morris Jacob.   "Political Attitudes of Ameri-
       can Women: A Study of the Effects of Work and
       Education on Their Political Role." Ph. D. disser-
       tation, University of Maryland, 1965.

1281   McCarthy, Amy.   "The Women's Trade Union League,
       1909-13." Ph. D. dissertation, Vassar College,
       1971.

1282   McCourt, Kathleen.   "Women and Grass-Roots Poli-
       tics: A Case Study of Working-Class Women's
       Participation in Assertive Community Organiza-
       tions." Ph. D. dissertation, University of Chicago,
       1975.

1283 Melder, Keith. "The Beginnings of the Women's Movement, 1800-1840." Ph. D. dissertation, Yale University, 1963.

1284 Meyers, Joel. "A Reputational Study of Woman Leadership in New Orleans." Master's thesis, Tulane University, 1971.

1285 Minnis, Mhyra S. "The Relationship of Women's Organizations to the Social Structure of a City." Ph. D. dissertation, Yale University, 1951.

1286 Morrissey, William. "The Status and Perceptions of Women School Board Members in Indiana." Ph. D. dissertation, Indiana University, 1972.

1287 Paget, Karen M. "A Woman in Politics: Change in Role Perceptions." Ph. D. dissertation, University of Colorado, 1975.

1288 Richards, Catherine V. "A Study of Class Differences in Women's Participation." D. S. W. dissertation, Case Western Reserve University, 1958.

1289 Rosenberg, Marie Barovic. "Women in Politics: A Comparative Study of Congresswomen Edith Green and Julia Butler Hansen." Ph. D. dissertation, University of Washington, 1973.

1290 Rosenfeld, Raymond A. "Points of Coalescence of Voluntary Organizations: Desegregation in Atlanta." Ph. D. dissertation, Emory University, 1973.

1291 Schaffer, Ronald. "Jeanette Rankin." Ph. D. dissertation, Princeton University, 1959.

1292 Shanley, Robert. "The League of Women Voters: A Study of Pressure Politics in the Public Interest." Ph. D. dissertation, Georgetown University, 1955.

1293 Stelzer, Leigh. "The Receptivity of School Board Members: A Study of the Requisites of Representation." Ph. D. dissertation, University of Michigan, 1971.

1294 Strayer, Richard Levi. "An Analysis of the Factors Resulting in the Social Composition of the Public

Boards of Education in Selected School Districts."
Ph. D. dissertation, Temple University, 1966.

1295   Tomkins, Jean Beattie.   "A Study of Women's Volun-
       tary Association Behavior."   Ph. D. dissertation,
       University of Iowa, 1955.

1296   Van Hightower, Nikki.   "Women Politicians: Social
       Backgrounds, Self-Concepts and Sex-Role Stereo-
       types."   Ph. D. dissertation, New York University,
       1974.

1297   Wells, Audrey Siess.   "Female Attitudes Toward Wo-
       men in Politics: The Propensity to Support Women."
       Ph. D. dissertation, University of Florida, 1972.

1298   Zellman, Gail Lemerman.   "Sex Roles and Political
       Socialization."   Ph. D. dissertation, University of
       California at Los Angeles, 1973.

1299   Zimmerman, Loretta Ellen.   "Alice Paul and the
       National Woman's Party, 1912-1920."   Ph. D. dis-
       sertation, Tulane University, 1964.

UNPUBLISHED PAPERS
PRESENTED AT PROFESSIONAL MEETINGS

1300 Amundsen, Kirsten. "The Ideology of Sexism and Its
       Victims in American Politics." Paper presented
       at the annual meeting of the Western Political
       Science Association, 1971.

1301 _____. "Social Policy Issues Affecting Women's
       Political Roles." Paper presented at the annual
       meeting of the American Association for the Ad-
       vancement of Science, 1974.

1302 Andrew, Jean Douglas. "Constance Baker Motley:
       Black, Female and Successful: Assets and Lia-
       bilities." Paper presented at the annual meeting
       of the American Political Science Association,
       1974.

1303 Arrington, Theodore S., and Kyle, Patricia A. "Equal
       Rights Amendment Activists in North Carolina."
       Paper presented at the annual meeting of the
       American Political Science Association, 1975.

1304 Barr, Donna M.; Walker, N. Darlene; and Durand,
       Roger. "Popular View of Feminist Politics."
       Paper presented at the annual meeting of the South-
       western Social Science Association, 1976.

1305 Beck, Audrey P. "Women and Power." Paper pre-
       sented at the Connecticut Conference of the Women's
       Political Caucuses, 1973.

1306 Benedict, Kennette. "Participatory Democracy in the
       Feminist Movement: A Case Study of the Palo
       Alto Women's Coalition." Paper presented at the
       annual meeting of the American Political Science
       Association, 1976.

1307   Bers, Trudy Haffron. "Local Political Elites: Men
        and Women on Boards of Education." Paper pre-
        sented at the annual meeting of the Southern Politi-
        cal Science Association, 1976.

1308   Boneparth, Ellen. "The Impact of Commissions on
        the Status of Women on the Policy Making Process:
        A California Case Study." Paper presented at the
        annual meeting of the American Political Science
        Association, 1976.

1309   Bourque, Susan C., and Grossholtz, Jean. "Political
        Participation, Sex and Politics: From the Bedroom
        to the Barricades." Paper presented at the annual
        meeting of the American Political Science Associa-
        tion, 1973.

1310   _____, _____. "Politics as an Unnatural Prac-
        tice: Political Science Looks at Female Partici-
        pation." Paper presented at the annual meeting of
        the American Political Science Association, 1973.

1311   Bozeman, Barry; Thornton, Sandra; and McKinney,
        Michael. "Continuity and Change in Opinions About
        Sex Roles." Paper presented at the annual meeting
        of the Southwestern Political Science Association,
        1975.

1312   Brandmeyer, Gerald, and Stoudinger, Susan. "Sex
        Differentials in Student Political Behavior." Paper
        presented at the annual meeting of the Southern
        Sociological Society, 1974.

1313   Bromely, David; Kornberg, Allan; and Smith, Joel.
        "Variable Partisan Commitment Among Politically
        Active Women." Paper presented at the annual
        meeting of the Midwestern Political Science Asso-
        ciation, 1968.

1314   Bryan, Frank. "Comparative Town Meetings: A
        Search for Causative Models in Feminine Involve-
        ment in Politics." Paper presented at the annual
        meeting of the Rural Sociological Society, 1975.

1315   Burrell, Barbara. "A New Dimension in Political
        Participation: The Women's Political Caucus."
        Paper presented at the annual meeting of the South-
        western Social Science Association, 1975.

1316   Cannon, Ellen S. , and Talarico, Susette M.   "Women
           and Crime: A Study in Power. "   Paper presented
           at the annual meeting of the American Political
           Science Association, 1976.

1317   Card, Emily. "Organizing the National Women's
           Political Caucus in Orange County, California. "
           Paper presented at the annual meeting of the
           American Political Science Association, 1972.

1318   Christy, Carol. "The Political Participation of Women
           in Mass Industrial Societies. "   Paper presented at
           the annual meeting of the Ohio Association of Econo-
           mists and Political Scientists, 1974.

1319   Conway, M. Margaret. "Sex Differences in Children's
           Political Orientations: Continuity and Change. "
           Paper presented at the annual meeting of the
           Southern Political Science Association, 1976.

1320   _____, and Feigert, Frank B. "Motivations and
           Task Performance Among Party Precinct Workers. "
           Paper presented at the annual meeting of the Ameri-
           can Political Science Association, 1973.

1321   Corbett, A. Michael, and Frankland, Gene. "Sexism
           as a Function of Socio-economic, Psychological
           and Political Variables. "   Paper presented at the
           annual meeting of the Midwest Political Science
           Association, 1976.

1322   Costain, Anne N. "A Social Movement Lobbies:
           Women's Liberation and Pressure Politics. "
           Paper presented at the annual meeting of the
           Southern Political Science Association, 1975.

1323   Cowan, Ruth B. "Litigation as a Strategy in Women's
           Rights Politics: An Examination of the ACLU
           Women's Rights Project. "   Paper presented at the
           annual meeting of the American Political Science
           Association, 1975.

1324   _____. "Some Observations About Gender, Roles
           and Power. "   Paper presented at the Adelphi Uni-
           versity Conference on Women and Politics, 1975.

1325   _____. "Theoreticians of Power in the Women's

Movement." Paper presented at the annual meeting of the Midwest Political Science Association, 1976.

1326 Currey, Virginia. "Achieving the Female Share of the Political Plums - Is a Quota System Necessary?" Paper presented at the annual meeting of the Southwestern Sociological Association, 1973.

1327 _____. "Campaign Theory and Practice--The Gender Variable." Paper presented at the annual meeting of the Southwestern Political Science Association, 1975.

1328 Daniels, Arlene Kaplan. "Is There a Female Power Elite? Local and Cosmopolitan Networks in the United States." Paper presented at the annual meeting of the British Sociological Association, 1976.

1329 Darcy, R., and Schramm, Sarah S. "When Women Run Against Men: Voters' Response to Congressional Contests." Paper presented at the annual meeting of the Southern Political Science Association, 1975.

1330 _____, _____. "Woman Types: Differential Responses to Politics." Paper presented at the annual meeting of the Southern Political Science Association, 1976.

1331 Diamond, Irene. "Why Aren't They There?: Women in American State Legislatures." Paper presented at the annual meeting of the American Political Science Association, 1976.

1332 Durand, Roger; Barr, Donna M.; and Walker, Darlene. "Dimensions and Correlates of Attitudes Towards the Women's Movement." Paper presented at the annual meeting of the Western Political Science Association, 1976.

1333 Elshtain, Jean Bethke. "On Teaching Feminist Politics." Paper presented at the annual meeting of the American Political Science Association, 1974.

1334 Everett, Jana. "Woman's Movement Origins: Constraints and Opportunities." Paper presented at

the annual meeting of the Western Political Science
Association, 1976.

1335   Falik, Marilyn.   "The Impact of the Supreme Court
       Decision on Abortion: Political and Legislative
       Resistance v. Court Reactions."   Paper presented
       at the annual meeting of the American Political
       Science Association, 1974.

1336   Farah, Barbara G., and Sapiro, Virginia.   "New Pride
       and Old Prejudice: Political Ambition and Role
       Orientations Among Female Partisan Elites."   Paper
       presented at the annual meeting of the Southern
       Political Science Association, 1975.

1337   _____, _____.   "Where the Women Are: A
       Cross-time Study of Political Activists."   Paper
       presented at the annual meeting of the Midwest
       Political Science Association, 1976.

1338   _____, _____.   "The World of Longitudinal De-
       signs in the Study of Women Activists."   Paper
       presented at the annual meeting of the Southern
       Political Science Association, 1976.

1339   Farrell, Warren T.   "Women's and Men's Liberation
       Groups: Political Power Within the System and
       Outside the System."   Paper presented at the annual
       meeting of the American Political Science Associa-
       tion, 1971.

1340   Ferree, Myra Marx.   "Social Networks and the Dif-
       fusion of Feminism."   Paper presented at the annual
       meeting of the American Sociological Association,
       1976.

1341   Fiedler, Maureen.   "The Participation of Women in
       American Politics."   Paper presented at the annual
       meeting of the American Political Science Associa-
       tion, 1975.

1342   Flora, Cornelia Butler.   "Working Class Women's
       Political Participation: Its Potential in Developed
       Countries."   Paper presented at the annual meeting
       of the American Political Science Association, 1974.

1343   Franklin, Joan.   "Political Participation, Voluntary

Organization Membership, and Sex Differences:
An Examination of Relationships. " Paper presented
at the annual meeting of the American Political
Science Association, 1975.

1344 Freeman, Jo. "Conflicts and Crises of Social Movement Organizations. " Paper presented at the
Eastern Regional Conference of the National Organization for Women, Atlantic City, New Jersey,
September 1974.

1345 _____. "Political Organization in the Feminist
Movement. " Paper presented at the annual meeting
of the American Political Science Association, 1974.

1346 _____. "Women and Public Policy. " Paper presented at the annual meeting of the American
Political Science Association, 1975.

1347 Garretson, Lucy. "American Women in Politics:
Culture, Structure, and Ideology. " Paper presented at the 9th International Congress of Anthro-
pological and Ethnological Sciences, 1973.

1348 Gehlen, Frieda L. "Legislative Content Comparisons
between Males and Females in the United States
House of Representatives. " Paper presented at
the annual meeting of the Southwestern Social
Science Association, 1975.

1349 _____. "Women Members of Congress: A Distinctive Role. " Paper presented at the Southwestern
Social Science Meetings, 1972.

1350 _____. "Women Members of the U. S. House of
Representatives and Role Expectations. " Paper
presented at the annual meeting of the Ohio Valley
Sociological Society, 1967.

1351 Gelb, Joyce, and Sardell, Alice. "Strategies for the
Powerless: The Welfare Rights Movement in New
York City. " Paper presented at the annual meeting
of the American Political Science Association, 1973.

1352 Gillespie, Joanna B. "The Phenomenon of the Public
Wife. " Paper presented at the annual meeting of
the American Sociological Association, 1976.

1353   Gitelson, Alan R. , and Gitelson, Idy B.   "Reactions
        to Male and Female Success and Failure in Running
        for Political Office. " Paper presented at the annual
        meeting of the Southern Political Science Associa-
        tion, 1976.

1354   Githens, Marianne. "Spectators, Agitators, or Law-
        makers: Women in State Legislatures. " Paper
        presented at the annual meeting of the Southern
        Political Science Association, 1974.

1355   _____. "Women in Politics: Differences in Attitudes
        of Amateurs and Professionals - A Case Study. "
        Paper presented at the annual meeting of the South-
        western Social Science Association, 1975.

1356   Gruberg, Martin. "Women in Power: Is 1976 a Year
        of Erosion, Breakthrough, or Plateauing ?" Paper
        presented at the annual meeting of the American
        Political Science Association, 1976.

1357   Heide, Wilma Scott.   "Trends Affecting Volunteers
        Today: Feminist Perspective on Volunteering for
        a Healthy Society. " Paper presented at the annual
        meeting of the National Easter Seal Society, 1973.

1358   Hershey, Majorie Randon.   "The Politics of Androgyny ?
        Sex Roles and Attitudes Toward Women in Politics. "
        Paper presented at the annual meeting of the Mid-
        west Political Science Association, 1976.

1359   Hoag, Wendy, and Farah, Barbara G.   "Sex Differ-
        ences in Political Leadership. " Paper presented
        at the annual meeting of the Midwest Political
        Science Association, 1975.

1360   Huckle, Patricia, and Hall, Owen P.   "Strategies for
        Changing Employment of Women in Local Govern-
        ment. " Paper presented at the annual meeting of
        the American Political Science Association, 1972.

1361   Iglitzin, Lynne B.   "A Case Study in Patriarchal
        Politics: Women on Welfare. " Paper presented
        at the annual meeting of the American Political
        Science Association, 1973.

1362   _____.   "From Classroom to Smoke-Filled Room:

The Reality Gap." Paper presented at the annual
meeting of the Western Political Science Association, 1975.

1363   _____. "Sex-Typing and Politicization in Children's
Attitudes: Reflections on Studies Done and Undone."
Paper presented at the annual meeting of the
American Political Science Association, 1972.

1364   _____. "Teaching Political Science: A Feminist
Perspective." Paper presented at the annual
meeting of the American Political Science Association, 1976.

1365   Jaros, Dean. "Sex, Psychophysiology, and Political
Behavior." Paper presented at the annual meeting
of the Midwest Political Science Association, 1976.

1366   Johnson, Marilyn. "Changing Patterns of Voluntary
Affiliation in the Later Years." Paper presented
at the annual meeting of the American Sociological
Association, 1975.

1367   _____. "Exhibits: Secondary Analysis: Age, Sex
and Trends in Voluntary Activity." Tables pre-
pared for the Social Science Research Council
Sponsored Conference on the Meaning of Work,
Leisure and Retirement among Middle-Aged Women,
Russell Sage Foundation, New York, 1975.

1368   Johnson, Roberta, and Stoper, Emily. "The 'Superi-
ority' of Women--Passport to Power." Paper presented at the annual meeting of the Southwest
Political Science Association, 1976.

1369   Kanter, Rosabeth Moss. "Women and Hierarchies."
Paper presented at the annual meeting of the
American Sociological Association, 1975.

1370   Katznelson, Ira. "Participation and Political Buffers
in Urban America." Paper presented at the annual
meeting of the American Political Science Association, 1972.

1371   Keller, Suzanne. "Looking Ahead in the 1970's."
Paper presented at the Radcliffe Institute for
Women Conference "Women: Resource for a

Changing World. "   Cambridge, Massachusetts,
1972.

1372   Kincaid, Diane D.   "Over His Dead Body: A New
       Perspective and Some Feminist Footnotes on
       Widows in the U. S. Congress. "   Paper presented
       at the annual meeting of the American Political
       Science Association, 1976.

1373   King, Elizabeth G.   "Women in Iowa Legislative Poli-
       tics. "   Paper presented at the annual meeting of
       the American Political Science Association, 1973.

1374   _____, and McAuliffe, Joan.   "Women County
       Supervisors: Are They Different?"   Paper pre-
       sented at the annual meeting of the American
       Political Science Association, 1976.

1375   Kinnard, Cynthia.   "Political Anti-Feminism: From
       Anti-Suffrage to the 'Stop ERA' Movement. "   Paper
       presented at the Berkshire Conference on the
       History of Women, 1976.

1376   Kirkpatrick, Jeane.   "A New Breed: Delegate Incen-
       tives and Role Perceptions at the 1972 Conventions. "
       Paper presented at the annual meeting of the South-
       western Social Science Association, 1975.

1377   Knutson, Jeanne N.   "Long Term Effects of Person-
       ality on Political Attitudes and Beliefs. "   Paper
       presented at the annual meeting of the American
       Political Science Association, 1973.

1378   Krauss, Wilma Rule.   "U. S. State Environments and
       Women's Recruitment to State Legislatures and
       Congress. "   Paper presented at the annual meeting
       of the American Political Science Association, 1975.

1379   _____.   "Women in Parliament and Local Politics:
       A Cross-National Comparison of Recruitment
       Patterns. "   Paper presented at the annual meeting
       of the Midwest Political Science Association, 1974.

1380   Kuehn, Lucille.   "American Voluntarism: An Anti-
       history with Anti-heroines. "   Paper presented at
       the Radcliffe Institute for Women Conference
       "Women: Resource for a Changing World. "   Cam-
       bridge, Massachusetts, 1972.

1381 Kyle, Patricia A. "Socialization and Recruitment
      Patterns of Women in Party Elite Positions in
      North Carolina." Paper presented at the annual
      meeting of the American Political Science Asso-
      ciation, 1974.

1382 Lansing, Majorie. "The Political Behavior of British
      and American Women." Paper presented at the
      annual meeting of the American Political Science
      Association, 1976.

1383 _____. "Sex Differences in Activism and Voting."
      Paper presented at the annual meeting of the
      American Political Science Association, 1971.

1384 _____. "The Voting Patterns of American Black
      Women." Paper presented at the annual meeting
      of the American Political Science Association,
      1973.

1385 Leahy, Peter J. "Mobilization and Recruitment of
      Leadership to Anti-abortion Movement: A Test of
      Some Hypotheses." Paper presented at the annual
      meeting of the Southwestern Social Science Asso-
      ciation, 1976.

1386 Lee, Marcia Manning. "The Participation of Women
      as Compared to Men in Local Public Office and
      Party Leadership Positions." Paper presented at
      the annual meeting of the American Political Science
      Association, 1974.

1387 _____. "Towards Understanding Why Few Women
      Hold Public Office: Factors Affecting the Partici-
      pation of Women in Local Politics." Paper pre-
      sented at the annual meeting of the American
      Political Science Association, 1974.

1388 Lipetz, Marcia J. "Participation in the Woman's
      Rights Movement: Sociologists and Working Class
      Women." Paper presented at the annual meeting
      of the Ohio Valley Sociological Society, 1972.

1389 Lynn, Naomi B., and Camin, Kathleen. "Tactics and
      Strategies of Organizing for Impact and Success."
      Paper presented at the annual meeting of the South-
      western Social Science Association, 1975.

1390 _____, and Flora, Cornelia B. "Child-Bearing and Political Participation: The Changing Sense of Self." Paper presented at the annual meeting of the American Political Science Association, 1972.

1391 _____, _____. "Societal Punishment and Aspects of Female Political Participation: 1972 National Convention Delegates." Paper presented at the annual meeting of the Southwestern Political Science Association, 1972.

1392 _____, _____. "Women Delegates to the National Convention: A Regional Perspective." Paper presented at the annual meeting of the Midwest Political Science Association, 1973.

1393 McCourt, Kathleen. "Grass Roots Politics and Working-Class Women." Paper presented at the annual meeting of the Midwest Political Science Association, 1975.

1394 _____. "Protest and Politics in Chicago: The Participation of Working Class Women in Assertive Community Organizations." Paper presented at the annual meeting of the Midwest Political Science Association, 1975.

1395 MacManus, Susan A. "Determinants of the Equitability of Female Representation on 243 City Councils." Paper presented at the annual meeting of the American Political Science Association, 1976.

1396 Matasar, Ann B., and Porter, Mary. "The Role and Status of Women in the Daley Organization." Paper presented at the annual meeting of the American Political Science Association, 1972.

1397 Merritt, Sharyne. "Recruitment and Role Perceptions of Suburban Officeholders." Paper presented at the annual meeting of the Midwest Political Science Association, 1976.

1398 Mezey, Susan Gluck. "Women Politicians and Women's Issues: The Case of Hawaii." Paper presented at the annual meeting of the American Political Science Association, 1976.

1399 Mitchell, Joyce M., and Starr, Rachel. "Aspirations,

Achievement and Professional Advancement in
Political Science: The Prospect for Women in the
West. " Paper presented at the annual meeting of
the Western Political Science Association, 1971.

1400   Murphy, Irene L. "The Impact of Women's Groups on
National Policy on the Status of Women. " Paper
presented at the annual meeting of the Northeastern
Political Science Association, 1973.

1401   _____. "Organized Groups and Political Activity. "
Paper presented at the annual meeting of the Northeastern Political Science Association, 1973.

1402   Nicholson, Jeanne Bell. "The Citizen's Commission
and the Executive Director: The Case of Local
Commissions for Women. " Paper presented at the
annual meeting of the Southern Political Science Association, 1976.

1403   Oliver, David. "The Social and Political Implications
of Being an Older Woman. " Paper presented at
the annual meeting of the Southwestern Social Science
Association, 1975.

1404   Olsen, Marvin E. "Interest Association Participation
and Political Activity in the United States and
Sweden. " Paper presented at the annual meeting
of the American Sociological Association, 1974.

1405   Pilant, Denny. "Sexual Due Process and the Supreme
Court. " Paper presented at the annual meeting of
the Southern Political Science Association, 1976.

1406   Prestage, Jewel, and Githens, Marianne. "Prototypes
in Marginality: Women in American Political
Life. " Paper presented at the annual meeting of
the Southwestern Social Science Association, 1976.

1407   Ramirez, Francisco O. ; Weiss, Jane A. ; and Tracy,
Terry. "The Political Incorporation of Women:
A Cross-National Analysis. " Paper presented at
the annual meeting of the American Sociological
Association, 1975.

1408   Raphael, Edna E. "From Sewing Machines to Politics: The Woman Union Member in the Community. "

Paper presented at the annual meeting of the Society for the Study of Social Problems, 1973.

1409 Rathjen, Gregory J., and Kay, Susan Ann. "The Impact of Sex Differences on the Attitudes and Beliefs of Appellate Lawyers." Paper presented at the annual meeting of the Southern Political Science Association, 1975.

1410 Richard, Patricia Bayer. "Cool, Lukewarm, Hot-- Degress of Movement Participation." Paper presented at the annual meeting of the Southwestern Social Science Association, 1976.

1411 _____. "Participation in the Women's Movement: Who Does It and Why?" Paper presented at the annual meeting of the Midwest Political Science Association, 1976.

1412 Rogers, David, et al. "Voluntary Association Membership and Political Participation - an Exploration of the Mobilization Hypothesis." Paper presented at the annual meeting of the Midwest Sociology Society, 1974.

1413 Rosenberg, Marie Barovic. "Political Efficacy and Sex Role: Case Study of Congresswomen Edith Green and Julia Butler Hansen." Paper presented at the annual meeting of the American Political Science Association, 1972.

1414 Rothschild, Joan. "Female Power: A Marxist-Feminist Perspective." Paper presented at the annual meeting of the American Political Science Association, 1976.

1415 _____. "On Building a Female Constituency. The Case of Massachusetts." Paper presented at the annual meeting of the American Political Science Association, 1972.

1416 Sapiro, Virginia. "Three Models of Women and Politics in Normative Political Theory: Toward Elimination of Straw Pigs." Paper presented at the annual meeting of the American Political Science Association, 1976.

1417 Schramm, Sarah Slavin. "Issues About Methodology in

the Study of Women and Politics." Paper presented at the annual meeting of the American Political Science Association, 1976.

1418 Scott, Ruth. "Non-Elites: The Basis of Acceptance."
      Paper presented at the annual meeting of the
      American Political Science Association, 1973.

1419 Sells, Lucy W. "On Increasing Political Effective-
      ness." Paper presented at the annual convention
      of the National Women's Political Caucus of Cali-
      fornia, 1973.

1420 Sigel, Roberta. "The Adolescent in Politics: The
      Case of American Girls." Paper presented at the
      annual meeting of the American Political Science
      Association, 1975.

1421 Smith, Leticia. "Women and the Double Subsidy: A
      Feminist Re-evaluation of Volunteerism." Paper
      presented at the annual meeting of the Midwest
      Sociological Society, 1974.

1422 Soule, John W., and McGrath, Wilma E. "A Compara-
      tive Study of Male-Female Political Attitudes at
      Citizen and Elite Levels." Paper presented at the
      annual meeting of the American Political Science
      Association, 1974.

1423 Stiehm, Judith, and Scott, Ruth. "Female and Male:
      Voluntary and Chosen Participation. Sex, SES,
      and Participation." Paper presented at the annual
      meeting of the American Political Science Associa-
      tion, 1974.

1424 Stoper, Emily, and Johnson, Roberta. "The Weaker
      Sex and the Better Half." Paper presented at the
      annual meeting of the Western Political Science
      Association, 1976.

1425 Tedin, Kent L. "Religious Preference and Pro/Anti
      Activism on the Equal Rights Amendment Issue."
      Paper presented at the annual meeting of the
      Southern Political Science Association, 1976.

1426 Thomas, Mary Jean. "Mercy Otis Warren: Her Role
      in the Campaign Leading to the American Revolution."

Paper presented at the annual meetings of the
Speech Communication Association, 1974; Midwest
Political Science Association, 1975; and University
and College Women of Illinois, 1975.

1427 Tolchin, Susan. "The Exclusion of Women from the
      Judicial Selection Process." Paper presented at
      the annual meeting of the American Political
      Science Association, 1975.

1428 Trent, Judith S., and Trent, Jimmie D. "The Na-
      tional Women's Political Caucus: A Rhetorical
      Biography." Paper presented at the annual meeting
      of the Eastern Communication Association, 1973.

1429 Tresemer, D., and Pleck, J. H. "Maintaining and
      Changing Sex-Role Boundaries in Men (and Women)."
      Paper presented at the Radcliffe Institute for Women
      Conference "Women: Resources for a Changing
      World." Cambridge, Massachusetts, 1972.

1430 Van Hightower, Nikki. "The Recruitment of Women
      for Public Office." Paper presented at the annual
      meeting of the Southwestern Social Science Asso-
      ciation, 1976.

1431 Venning, Corey B. "Women's Silence and the Failure
      of Political Thought." Paper presented at the
      annual meeting of the Midwest Political Science As-
      sociation, 1975.

1432 Wanat, Susan. "The ERA: Its Impact on State Legis-
      lation and the Status of Women." Paper presented
      at the annual meeting of the Midwest Political
      Science Association, 1973.

1433 Weisman, Martha. "How Women in Politics View the
      Role Their Sex Plays in the Impact of Their
      Speeches on Audiences." Paper presented at the
      annual meeting of the Eastern Communication Asso-
      ciation, 1973.

1434 Wells, Audrey Siess, and Smeal, Eleanor. "Women's
      Attitudes toward Women in Politics: A Survey of
      Urban Registered Voters and Party Committee-
      women." Paper presented at the annual meeting of
      the American Political Science Association, 1972.

1435   Werner, Emmy, and Bachtold, Louise M.   "Personality
       Characteristics of Women in American Politics."
       Paper presented at the annual meeting of the Ameri-
       can Political Science Association, 1972.

1436   Whaley, Sara Stauffer.   "A Cross-National Review of
       Studies on the Status of Women."   Paper presented
       at the annual meeting of the American Political
       Science Association, 1973.

1437   Young, Louise.   "The Political Role of Women in the
       United States."   Paper presented at the annual
       meeting of the Hague Congress of International
       Political Science Association, 1952.

MISCELLANEOUS
UNPUBLISHED PAPERS

1438 Bernstein, Susan, and Brooks, Pamela. "Where Have
All the Women Gone?: Training Women in Public
Affairs, Results and Directions." Mimeographed.
San Francisco: Coro Foundation, 1971.

1439 Bers, Trudy Haffron. "Towards Understanding Differences Among Female Political Elites." Mimeographed. Morton Grove, Ill.: Oakton Community
College, Department of Political Science.

1440 _____. "Women in Nonpartisan Politics: The Case
of Suburban School Boards." Mimeographed.
Morton Grove, Ill.: Oakton Community College,
Department of Political Science.

1441 _____. "Women in Suburban Nonpartisan Office:
Who They Are and Where They're Going." Mimeo-
graphed. Morton Grove, Ill.: Oakton Community
College, Department of Political Science.

1442 Black, Charlene. "Leadership in Women's Voluntary
Associations: The Auxiliary as a Case in Point."
Mimeographed. Statesboro, Ga.: Georgia Southern
College, 1972.

1443 Bouxsein, Sandra, and Lansing, Marjorie. "Some
Determinants of the Political Behavior of British
and American Women." Mimeographed. Ann
Arbor: University of Michigan, 1974.

1444 Briggs, Thomas L. "Social Work Manpower Develop-
ments and Dilemmas of the 1970's." Mimeographed.
Syracuse, N.Y.: Syracuse University, School of
Social Work, Division of Continuing Education and
Manpower Development, 1972.

1445   Briscoe, J. B.   "Backgrounds of Women in Politics."
       Mimeographed.   Stockton, Calif.:   University of
       the Pacific, Department of Political Science, 1974.

1446   Brodsky, Jane.   "Woman Is a Political Animal: An
       Inquiry into the Depoliticization of the American
       Woman."   1973.   (Collection of the Center for the
       American Woman and Politics)

1447   Burns, Ruth Ann.   "State Senator Alene Ammond and
       the Press: The Key to Her Kingdom."   (Collec-
       tion of the Center for the American Woman and
       Politics)

1448   Camhi, Jane M.   "Women Against Women: A Study
       of Antifeminism in Action."   Mimeographed.   Med-
       ford, Mass.:   Tufts University, n. d.

1449   Coppock, Marjorie.   "The Extent and Political Impact
       of Women's Voluntary Activities."   Mimeographed.
       Syracuse, N. Y.:   Syracuse University, 1974.

1450   "Cornell Conference on Women" (22-25 January 1969).
       ($2.50, Sheila Tobias, Day Hall, Cornell Uni-
       versity, Ithaca, N. Y.   14850)

1451   Daniels, Arlene Kaplan.   "Development of a Female
       Power Elite in Urban Settings."   Mimeographed.
       Evanston, Ill.:   Northwestern University, Depart-
       ment of Sociology, 1976.

1452   _____.   "Room at the Top: Contingencies in a
       Voluntary Career."   Mimeographed.   Evanston,
       Ill.:   Northwestern University, Department of
       Sociology, 1976.

1453   Democratic Farm Labor Party.   "Women in the DFL
       ... A Preliminary Report: Present But Power-
       less?"   Mimeographed.   May, 1971.   (Koryne
       Horbal, State Chairwoman, 730 East 38th Street,
       Minneapolis, Minn.   55407)

1454   Demos, Vasilikie.   "Female Role Orientation and
       Participation in a Woman's Voluntary Association."
       Mimeographed.   South Bend, Ind.:   University of
       Notre Dame, n. d.

1455   DiCanio, Margaret.   "Paradoxes to Be Juggled in

Organizing Womanpower." Mimeographed. Memphis, Tenn.: Memphis State University, n.d.

1456 Dodge, Dorothy. "Career Goals and Attitudes of Undergraduate College Women." Mimeographed. St. Paul, Minn.: Macalester College, 1973.

1457 Eisenstein, Zillah R. "Women and Work Life: Conceptions of Social and Political Consciousness." Mimeographed. Boston: University of Massachusetts, n.d.

1458 Equitable Life Assurance Society of America. "Voluntarism among Equitable People." Mimeographed. New York: Equitable Life Assurance Society, 1973.

1459 Fengler, Alfred P. "Women in State Politics: Why So Few?" Mimeographed. Middlebury, Vt.: Middlebury College, n.d.

1460 Ferrandino, Marilyn. "Feminism as a Political Philosophy." Mimeographed. Tampa, Fla.: University of Southern Florida, Women's Studies Program.

1461 Fraser, Clara. "Which Road Towards Women's Liberation: the Movement as a Radical Vanguard or a Single-Issue Coalition?" Seattle: Radical Women, 1973.

1462 _____. "Woman as Leader: Double Jeopardy on Account of Sex." Seattle: Radical Women, 1972.

1463 Friedman, Susan Schuller. "A Study of the Emergence of a Social Movement: The Feminist Movement, 1960's and 1970's." 1974. (Collection of the Center for the American Woman and Politics)

1464 Gipple, Cindy. "The Women's Movement and the Class Struggle." Seattle: Radical Women, 1973.

1465 Githens, Marianne. "The Significance of Reference Groups: The League of Women Voters and Women Elected Officials." Mimeographed. Baltimore, Md.: Goucher College, Department of Political Science.

1466 Gold, Doris. "The Economics of Volunteerism."

1974.   (89-25 187th Street, Hollis, Queens, N. Y.
11423)

1467   Gruberg, Martin.   "Official Commissions on the Status
of Women: A Worldwide Movement. "   Mimeo-
graphed.   Oshkosh, Wis.:   University of Wisconsin,
n. d.

1468   Hallmark, Bob, and Savin, Adina.   "A National Survey
of Women Legislators. "   Mimeographed.   New
Brunswick, N. J.:   Rutgers University, Eagleton
Institute of Politics, 1971.

1469   Hammond, Nancy, and Hellman, Mary.   "Women's
Issues in the Legislature.   Michigan Legislative
Report 1971-72. "   Mimeographed.   (Michigan Wo-
men's Political Caucus, 1169 Sabron Drive, East
Lansing, Mich.   48823)

1470   Lambert, Kendall King, and Preston, James D.
"Women's Liberation: A Catalyst for Social
Change. "   Mimeographed.   Memphis, Tenn.:
Memphis State University.

1471   Lansing, Marjorie.   "Black Female Voters - New
Data. "   Mimeographed.   Ypsilanti, Mich.:   Eastern
Michigan University.

1472   Lee, Marcia Manning.   "Why Few Women Hold Public
Office: The Incompatibility of Democracy and
Traditional Sexual Role Assignments. "   Mimeo-
graphed.   Newark, N. J.:   Rutgers University,
Department of Political Science.

1473   _____.   "Women in Politics and Local Government. "
Mimeographed.   Newark, N. J.:   Rutgers University,
Department of Political Science.

1474   Lipman-Blumen, Jean, and Tickamyer, Ann.   "Sex
Roles in Transition: A Ten-Year Perspective. "
Mimeographed.   Washington, D. C.:   National
Institute of Education, Women's Research Staff,
n. d.

1475   Lynn, Naomi B.   "An Overview of the Involvement of
Women in American Politics: The Circumstances
of Their Participation. "   Mimeographed.   Manhattan,
Kans.:   Kansas State University, 1972.

1476   McFadden, Judith Nies. "Women on Capitol Hill."
        Mimeographed. Washington, D. C.: American
        Political Science Association, Committee on the
        Status of Women, 1972.

1477   "The Majority Wins: How to Build a Program for
        Legislative Change." 1974. (Box 954, Lansing,
        Mich. 48901, $2.10)

1478   Mayes, Sharon S. "Women in Positions of Authority:
        A Case Study of Changing Sex Roles." Mimeo-
        graphed. College Park, Md.: University of
        Maryland.

1479   Merritt, Sharyne. "Political Women and Political
        Men: Sex Differences in Motivations and Adapta-
        tions of Elected Local Political Officials." Mimeo-
        graphed. Park Forest South, Ill.: Governors
        State University, College of Cultural Studies, 1975.

1480   Miller, Vivian. "The National Committeewoman:
        Results of a Mail Survey." Mimeographed.
        Washington, D. C.: American Political Science
        Association, Committee on the Status of Women,
        1972.

1481   Murphy, H. "The Political Attitudes of Women."
        Mimeographed. Santa Clara, Calif.: University
        of Santa Clara, 1975.

1482   Paizis, Suzanne. "The Political Woman's Handbook."
        1973. (P. O. Box 943, Aptos, Calif. 94003,
        $2.50)

1483   _____. Politics: A Practical Handbook. (AAUW,
        Livermore-Pleasanton Branch, P. O. Box 661,
        Livermore, Calif. 94550, $1.25)

1484   Pohl, Joan R. "Women and the Political Milieu in
        Southern California, 1974." (Collection of the
        Center for the American Woman and Politics)

1485   Rosenberg, Marie Barovic. "Affirmative Action--
        Equal Employment Opportunity: Evolving Public
        Policy." Madison, Wisc.: University of Wisconsin-
        Extension, Institute of Governmental Affairs,
        1975.

1486   . "Women in Politics: Participation in
          Chippewa and Eau Claire Counties." Madison,
          Wis.: University of Wisconsin-Extension, Institute
          of Governmental Affairs, 1975.

1487   Rothschild, Joan. "On Building a Female Constituency:
          The Case of Massachusetts." Boston: Women's
          Research Center of Boston, 1972-1973.

1488   Segal, Phyllis. "Women and Political Parties: The
          Legal Dimension of Discrimination." Mimeographed.
          Washington, D.C.: American Political Science As-
          sociation, Committee on the Status of Women, 1972.

1489   Shaffer, Helen B. "Women's Consciousness Raising."
          Editorial Research Reports 2, 1973. (Editorial
          Research Reports, 1735 K Street, Washington,
          D.C. 20006)

1490   Smith, Marion. "Women in Pennsylvania Local Govern-
          ment." Mimeographed. Shippensburg, Pa.:
          Shippensburg State College, Center for Local and
          State Government, 1976.

1491   Stoneburner, Carol. "An Exploration of Four Leisure
          Life-Styles for Women." Mimeographed. Greens-
          boro, N.C.: University of North Carolina, Con-
          tinuing Education Guidance Center, 1972.

1492   Suelzle, Maryjean. "The Politics of the Equal Rights
          Amendment." Mimeographed. Berkeley, Calif.:
          University of California, Department of Sociology.

1493   Szalai, Alexander. "The Situation of Women in the
          United Nations." 1973. (United Nations Institute
          for Training and Research, Publications Section,
          801 U.N. Plaza, New York, N.Y. 10017)

1494   Tobias, Sheila. "Women's Liberation Phase Two."
          (Collection of the Center for the American Woman
          and Politics)

1495   Tulsa, Jacqueline Balk. "Historical Highlights and
          Quotations: Bibliography and Resources for Politi-
          cal Women." Mimeographed. Washington, D.C.:
          National Women's Political Caucus.

1496 Ario, Lois. "Assemblymen and Councilmen: Women
Legislators in Indiana." Ph. D. dissertation, University of Minnesota, in progress.

1497 Berson, Lenora. "The Role of Volunteer Women in
Philadelphia Party Politics." Center for the
American Woman and Politics, Florence Eagleton
Grants Program, 1974-75. Research in progress.

1498 Bouxsein, Sandra. "Attitudes and Background of the
League of Women Voters." Ph. D. dissertation,
The University of Michigan, Ann Arbor, Depart-
ment of Psychology, in progress.

1499 Bozeman, Barry; Thornton, Sandra; and McKinney,
Michael. "Continuity and Change in Opinions about
Sex Roles." In A Portrait of Marginality: The
Political Behavior of the American Woman, edited
by Marianne Githens and Jewel L. Prestage.
New York: David McKay, forthcoming, 1977.

1500 Braganza, Agnes. "Women in Leadership Roles:
Factors Influencing Virginia Women to Be or Not
to Be Candidates for Town and City Councils."
(105 Mare Ravine Road, Yorktown, Va. 23692.)
Research in progress.

1501 Bryce, Herrington J., and Warrick, Alan. "Black
Women in Electoral Politics." In A Portrait of
Marginality: The Political Behavior of the Ameri-
can Woman, edited by Marianne Githens and Jewel
L. Prestage. New York: David McKay, forth-
coming, 1977.

1502 Bullock, Charles S., and Heys, Patricia Findley.
"Recruitment of Women for Congress: A Research
Note." In A Portrait of Marginality: The Political

133

Behavior of the American Woman, edited by Marianne Githens and Jewel L. Prestage. New York:
David McKay, forthcoming, 1977.

1503   Burrell, Barbara. "A New Dimension in Political
Participation: The Women's Political Caucus."
In A Portrait of Marginality: The Political Be-
havior of the American Woman, edited by Marianne
Githens and Jewel L. Prestage. New York: David
McKay, forthcoming, 1977.

1504   Carroll, Susan. "An Analysis of Women Candidates
and Their Campaigns in the 1976 Primary Elections." Ph.D. dissertation, Indiana University,
in progress.

1505   Charlton, Sue Ellen M. "Participation and Attitudes
of Women in Colorado Politics." Colorado State
University, Fort Collins, Colo. Research in
progress.

1506   Cook, Beverly Blair. "The Opportunity Structure for
Women in Metropolitan Trial Courts." Center for
the American Woman and Politics, Florence Eagleton Grants Program, 1976-77. Research in
progress.

1507   Costain, Anne N. "Women's Lobbying: Political
Power in Voluntary Organizations." Center for
the American Woman and Politics, Florence
Eagleton Grants Program, 1974-75. Research in
progress.

1508   Costantini, Edmond, and Craik, Kenneth H. "Women
as Politicians: The Social Background, Personality,
and Political Careers of Female Party Leaders."
In A Portrait of Marginality: The Political Behavior of the American Woman, edited by Marianne
Githens and Jewel L. Prestage. New York: David
McKay, forthcoming, 1977.

1509   Cummings, Bernice, and Schuck, Victoria, eds. Untitled book about women and their struggle against
powerlessness. Garden City, L.I.: Adelphi University Press, forthcoming, 1977.

1510   Currey, Virginia. "Campaign Theory and Practice--

The Gender Variable." In A Portrait of Marginality: The Political Behavior of the American
Woman, edited by Marianne Githens and Jewel L.
Prestage. New York: David McKay, forthcoming,
1977.

1511 Cutler, Stephen. "A Longitudinal Analysis of Voluntary Association Participation among Middle-Aged
and Older Adults." Oberlin College, Ohio, Department of Sociology. Research in progress.

1512 Dillon, Mary, ed. Woman Power and Politics. New
York: Barrons Educational Series, forthcoming,
1977.

1513 Fee, Joan. Study of wives' and husbands' political
views and their organizational activity. National
Opinion Research Center, Chicago, Ill. Research
in progress.

1514 Flora, Cornelia Butler. "Working-Class Women's
Political Participation: Its Potential in Developed
Countries." In A Portrait of Marginality: The
Political Behavior of the American Woman, edited
by Marianne Githens and Jewel L. Prestage. New
York: David McKay, forthcoming, 1977.

1515 _____, and Lynn, Naomi B. "Women Delegates to
the 1972 Political Conventions." Kansas State University, Manhattan, Kans., Department of Sociology.
Research in progress.

1516 Gehlen, Frieda L. "Women Members of Congress:
A Distinctive Role." In A Portrait of Marginality:
The Political Behavior of the American Woman,
edited by Marianne Githens and Jewel L. Prestage.
New York: David McKay, forthcoming, 1977.

1517 Githens, Marianne. "Spectators, Agitators, or Lawmakers: Women in State Legislatures." In A
Portrait of Marginality: The Political Behavior of
the American Woman, edited by Marianne Githens
and Jewel L. Prestage. New York: David McKay,
forthcoming, 1977.

1518 _____, and Prestage, Jewel, eds. Portrait
of Marginality: The Political Behavior of the

American Woman. New York: David McKay, forthcoming, 1977.

1519   Harding, Rosemarie. "Black Women as Volunteers in the Afro-American Freedom Struggle: The Case of Ida B. Wells-Barnett." Center for the American Woman and Politics, Florence Eagleton Grants Program, 1974-75. Research in progress.

1520   Iglitzin, Lynne B. "A Cast Study in Patriarchal Politics: Women on Welfare." In A Portrait of Marginality: The Behavior of the American Woman, edited by Marianne Githens and Jewel L. Prestage. New York: David McKay, forthcoming, 1977.

1521   Johnson, Marilyn. "Local Officeholding and the Community: The Case of Women on New Jersey's School Boards." In untitled book about women and their struggle against powerlessness, edited by Bernice Cummings and Victoria Schuck. Garden City, L.I.: Adelphi University Press, forthcoming, 1977.

1522   King, Elizabeth G. "Women in Iowa Legislative Politics." In A Portrait of Marginality: The Political Behavior of the American Woman, edited by Marianne Githens and Jewel L. Prestage. New York: David McKay, forthcoming, 1977.

1523   King, Mae C. "The Politics of Sexual Stereotypes." In A Portrait of Marginality: The Political Behavior of the American Woman, edited by Marianne Githens and Jewel L. Prestage. New York: David McKay, forthcoming, 1977.

1524   Lansing, Majorie. "The Voting Patterns of American Black Women." In A Portrait of Marginality: The Political Behavior of the American Woman, edited by Marianne Githens and Jewel L. Prestage. New York: David McKay, forthcoming, 1977.

1525   Lee, Marcia M. "Toward Understanding Why Few Women Hold Public Office: Factors Affecting the Participation of Women in Local Politics." In A Portrait of Marginality: The Political Behavior of the American Woman, edited by Marianne Githens and Jewel L. Prestage. New York: David McKay, forthcoming, 1977.

1526   Lewis, Jan. "From Volunteer to Politician: A Com-
       parative Study of Black and White Politically Active
       Southern Women. " Center for the American Wo-
       man and Politics, Florence Eagleton Grants Pro-
       gram, 1974-75. Research in progress.

1527   Lex, Louise Ann Moede. "The Feminist Movement:
       Its Impact on Women in the State Legislatures. "
       Ph. D. dissertation, College of Education, Iowa
       State University, in progress.

1528   Lynn, Naomi B. , and Flora, Cornelia Butler. "So-
       cietal Punishment and Aspects of Female Political
       Participation: 1972 National Convention Delegates. "
       In A Portrait of Marginality: The Political Be-
       havior of the American Woman, edited by Mari-
       anne Githens and Jewel L. Prestage. New York:
       David McKay, forthcoming, 1977.

1529   Margolis, Diane. "Behavior in Political Places: A
       Study of Women and Men in Local Political Parties. "
       Center for the American Woman and Politics,
       Florence Eagleton Grants Program, 1974-75.
       Research in progress.

1530   Mathews, Jane De Hart, and Hobson, Roxie. "Southern
       Women and the Political Process: The Mobiliza-
       tion of North Carolina Women and the Fate of the
       ERA. " Center for the American Woman and Poli-
       tics, Florence Eagleton Grants Program, 1976-77.
       Research in progress.

1531   Merritt, Sharyne. "Women in Municipal Government:
       Cook County. " Center for the American Woman
       and Politics, Florence Eagleton Grants Program,
       1976-77. Research in progress.

1532   Mezey, Susan Gluck. "Women in Local Government:
       The Case of Connecticut. " Center for the Ameri-
       can Woman and Politics, Florence Eagleton Grants
       Program, 1976-77. Research in progress.

1533   Mueller, Marnie W. "A Study of the Economic De-
       terminants of Volunteer Work by Men and Women
       Based on Two Large National Samples. " Wesleyan
       University, Department of Economics. Research
       in progress.

1534 Musick-Jacobsen, Judith. A study of feminist orien-
      tation and political positions of women who served
      as delegates to the Democratic Convention in 1972.
      University of Oregon, Eugene, Oregon, Department
      of Sociology. Research in progress.

1535 National Opinion Research Center. "Politics and
      Families: Changing Role of Urban Women."
      National Opinion Research Center, Chicago, Ill.
      Research in progress.

1536 Nunn, Clyde, and Seifer, Nancy. "Social Change and
      Women: Results from National Surveys." Center
      for Policy Research, 475 Riverside Drive, New
      York, N.Y. 10027. Research in progress.

1537 Orum, Anthony, et al. "Sex, Socialization, and
      Politics." In A Portrait of Marginality: The
      Political Behavior of the American Woman, edited
      by Marianne Githens and Jewel L. Prestage. New
      York: David McKay, forthcoming, 1977.

1538 Pierce, John C.; Avery, William P.; and Carey,
      Addison, Jr. "Sex Differences in Black Political
      Beliefs and Behavior." In A Portrait of Margin-
      ality: The Political Behavior of the American
      Woman, edited by Marianne Githens and Jewel L.
      Prestage. New York: David McKay, forthcoming,
      1977.

1539 Prestage, Jewel. "Black Women State Legislators:
      A Profile." In A Portrait of Marginality: The
      Political Behavior of the American Woman, edited
      by Marianne Githens and Jewel L. Prestage. New
      York: David McKay, forthcoming, 1977.

1540 Reid, Inez Smith. "Traditional Political Animals? A
      Loud No." In A Portrait of Marginality: The
      Political Behavior of the American Woman, edited
      by Marianne Githens and Jewel L. Prestage. New
      York: David McKay, forthcoming, 1977.

1541 Soule, John W., and McGrath, Wilma E. "A Com-
      parative Study of Male-Female Political Attitudes
      at Citizen and Elite Levels." In A Portrait of
      Marginality: The Political Behavior of the Ameri-
      can Woman, edited by Marianne Githens and Jewel

L. Prestage. New York: David McKay, forthcoming, 1977.

1542 Starr, Rachael.   Study of the political recruitment
of women into public office with an analysis of
participation in voluntary organizations.   Ph. D.
dissertation, University of Oregon, Eugene, Oreg.,
Department of Political Science, in progress.

1543 Stewart, Debra W.   "A Comparative Analysis of Commissions on the Status of Women in Five Communities." Center for the American Woman and Politics, Florence Eagleton Grants Program, 1976-77.
Research in progress.

1544 Stone, Pauline.   Study of black women's political participation.   University of Michigan, Ann Arbor.
Research in progress.

1545 Stoper, Emily.   "Wife and Politician: Role Strain
Among Women in Public Office." In A Portrait
of Marginality: The Political Behavior of the
American Woman, edited by Marianne Githens and
Jewel L. Prestage. New York: David McKay,
forthcoming, 1977.

1546 Stucker, John J.   "Women as Voters: Their Matura-
tion as Political Persons in American Society."
In A Portrait of Marginality: The Political Be-
havior of the American Woman, edited by Marianne
Githens and Jewel L. Prestage. New York: David
McKay, forthcoming, 1977.

1547 West, Guida.   "The Welfare Rights Movement (1966-
1974): A Study of Coalition Politics." Ph. D.
dissertation, Rutgers University, New Brunswick,
N. J., Department of Sociology, in progress.

1548 Women's campaigns in 1976 co-directed by Ruth B.
Mandel (Center for the American Woman and Politics) and Betsey Wright (National Women's Education Fund). Research in progress.

AUTHOR INDEX

Burstein, P.   601
Butler, P.   99

- C -

Cade, T.   100
Calderwood, A.   417
California Commission on
   the Status of Women
   101
California Elected Women's
   Association for Educa-
   tion and Research   102
Calisher, H.   103
Calloway, D.   602
Camhi, J. M.   1448
Camin, K.   1389
Campbell, A.   104, 105,
   106, 107
Cannon, E. S.   1316
Cannon, J.   108
Cannon, M. W.   340
Cantril, A. H.   109
Cantril, S. D.   109
Card, E.   1317
Carden, M. L.   110
Carey, A. Jr.   1022, 1538
Carroll, S.   1252, 1504
Carter, L. J.   604
Carter, M. R.   111
Cartwright, M.   605
Cassara, B. B.   112
Cassell, J.   1253
Cater, L. A.   113
Cates, J. M. Jr.   606
Center for the American
   Woman and Politics
   4, 5, 35, 114, 115,
   116
Chafe, W.   117, 1254
Chamberlin, H.   118
Chandola, H.   607
Charlton, S. E. M.   1505
Chase, J.   608
Cheshire, H.   609
Cheshire, M.   609, 610

Chester, G.   119
Chisholm, S.   120, 121,
   611, 612, 613, 614,
   615, 616, 617
Chord, L. A.   618
Christy, C.   1318
Churchill, J. C.   619
Cimons, M.   601
Cisler, L.   6
Citizens Advisory Council
   on the Status of
   Women   122, 123
Clardy, M. L.   622
Coburn, J.   623
Coffin, T.   624
Cole, J. B.   7
Cole, M.   625
Coleman, R. P.   386
Collier, J. F.   626
Collins, H.   627
Colon, F. T.   628
Colorado Commission on
   the Status of Women
   124
Common Cause   125
Conference on the Role of
   the State Commissions
   on the Status of Women
   in Ten Western States,
   Portland, Ore.   126
Congressional Quarterly
   Editorial Research
   Reports   127
Connable, R.   631
Connell, E. T.   632
Conrad, E.   128
Conway, J.   633
Conway, M. M.   634,
   1319, 1320
Cook, A. H.   635
Cook, B. B.   1506
Coolidge, O. E.   130
Cooper, H. C.   104
Cooper, J.   131
Cooper, S. M.   131
Cope, S. D.   1
Coppock, M.   1449

_____. Congress. Senate.
Subcommittee on Re-
ports, Accounting,
and Management
1158
_____. Department of
Commerce. Bureau
of the Census 483
_____. Department of
Labor 484
_____. _____. Man-
power Administration
485, 486
_____. _____. Women's
Bureau 26, 487,
488, 489, 490, 491,
492
_____. Department of
State 493
_____. Interdepartmental
Committee on the
Status of Women
494
_____. Library of Con-
gress. Legislative
Reference Service
27
_____. President's Com-
mission on the Status
of Women 495, 496

- V -

Van De Riet, H. K. 730,
731
Van Helden, M. 497, 498
Van Hightower, N. 1296,
1430
Van Riper, P. P. 499
Vaughan, D. S. 1159
Venning, C. B. 1431
Verba, S. 62, 500
Viorst, J. 1161
Virden, H. 1162
Volgy, S. S. 1164
Volgy, T. J. 1164

- W -

Wahlke, J. C. 501
Wai-hing Lo, H. 28
Wakefield, D. 1165
Walker, D. 1332
Walker, L. C. 502
Walker, N. D. 1304
Wallace, D. 503
Walter, B. O. 850
Walter, L. M. 1166
Walters, R. 1167
Wanat, S. 1432
Ware, C. 504
Warrick, A. 593, 594,
1501
Watkins, M. 505
Webb, G. E. 726
Weinberg, B. 1168
Weiner, R. 324
Weir, E. T. 1169
Weis, J. M. 1170
Weisman, M. 1433
Weiss, J. A. 1407
Weiss, R. S. 1171
Weitzman, L. J. 1172
Wellisch, K. 55
Wells, A. S. 1173, 1297,
1434
Wells, M. W. 506
Werner, E. 1174, 1175,
1176, 1435
Wertheimer, B. M. 507
Wery, M. K. 25a
West, G. 1547
Westoff, L. A. 1177
Weston, M. 1178
Wexford, M. 11
Whaley, S. S. 29, 1436
Wheeler, H. 30, 31
White, J. B. 1185
White, M. L. 1186
White, T. H. 508
White, W. S. 1187
Whitton, M. O. 509,
1188
Wiener, R. 1191

BIOGRAPHICAL INDEX

The following three books include biographies
of women who have served in Congress.
These books are not included in the index
under the Congresswoman's name.

Chamberlin, Hope. A Minority of Members:
Women in the U.S. Congress. New York:
Praeger, 1973.

Engelbarts, Rudolf. Women in the United States
Congress: 1917-1972. Littleton, Colo.: Libraries Unlimited, 1974.

Tolchin, Susan. Women in Congress: 1917-
1976. Washington, D.C.: U.S. Government
Printing Office, 1976.